sushi

sushi

easy recipes for making sushi at home

Emi Kazuko, Fiona Smith, Elsa Petersen-Schepelern

RYLAND

PETERS

& SMALL

LONDON NEW YORK

First published in Great Britain in 2006
Ryland Peters & Small
20–21 Jockey's Fields
London WC1R 4BW
www.rylandpeters.com
10 9 8 7 6 5 4 3 2 1

Text © Emi Kazuko, Fiona Smith,
Elsa Petersen-Schepelern 2006
Design and photographs
© Ryland Peters & Small 2006

ISBN-10: 1 84597 096 9
ISBN-13: 978 1 84597 096 3

A CIP catalogue record for this book is available
from the British Library.
Printed in China

Notes
• All spoon measurements are level unless otherwise
noted.
• Eggs are medium unless otherwise specified. Raw
fish or shellfish and uncooked or partly cooked eggs
should not be served to the very old, frail, young
children, pregnant women or those with compromised
immune systems.

Designer Luana Gobbo
Commissioning Editor
   Elsa Petersen-Schepelern
Production Gavin Bradshaw
Picture Research Tracy Ogino
Art Director Anne-Marie Bulat
Editorial Director Julia Charles

Food Stylists Emi Kazuko, Lucie McKelvie,
   Sunil Vijayakar, Linda Tubby
Prop Stylists Wei Tang, Hélène Lesur,
   Mary Norden
Index Hilary Bird

contents

introduction

Sushi has come a long way in a relatively short time. It is amazing that the mystique surrounding this style of food kept it from being a favourite with home cooks for so long.

But how things have changed! Fresh sushi can be found everywhere from restaurants to supermarkets and fast-food outlets. It is served at elegant parties or the simplest home gatherings. Travel-weary tourists choose sushi restaurants for comforting, familiar food. Children have it in their lunchboxes, and even some school canteens serve it. Sushi has become this generation's healthy convenience food.

Techniques used in making sushi can be simplified for the home cook. One of the most popular styles, rolled sushi (*maki-zushi*), is easy and fun to make at home and, as soon as the process of rolling the rice has been mastered, a world of filling options becomes available. These days, our supermarkets are full of all kinds of sushi ingredients.

SUSHI-MAKING UTENSILS AND INGREDIENTS

Special sushi-making utensils and authentic ingredients are beautiful and useful, and sold even in supermarkets. Many brands of nori are available pretoasted and in a variety of grades – use the best you can.

Some of the recipes in this book call for only half a sheet. When this is so, cut the sheets in half from the shortest side, so you are left with the most width. When making rolled sushi remember that rice is easier to handle with wet hands and it is better to handle nori with dry. Keep a bowl of vinegared water and a towel on hand to make the job easier.

SERVING SUSHI

Traditional accompaniments for sushi are soy sauce, wasabi paste and pickled ginger, and it is often served with miso soup. A smear of wasabi can elevate a piece of sushi from the ordinary to something extraordinary.

If you do not want to add wasabi in the sushi, serve a small mound on the side, or serve the sushi with a small dish of plain soy and one of wasabi and soy mixed together. Bought wasabi varies immensely; it is possible to find paste with a high percentage of real wasabi, but many are mostly horseradish – once again, buy the best you can or make your own (page 124).

Sushi is traditionally served immediately, but if you have to keep it for a while, wrap uncut rolls in clingflm. Keep in a cool place, but NOT in the refrigerator, which will make the rice hard and unpleasant – the vinegar in the rice will help to preserve it for a short time.

ingredients

shoyu
(Japanese soy sauce)

mirin
(Japanese sweet rice wine, for cooking only)

su
(Japanese rice vinegar)

sake
(Japanese rice wine)

nori
(sheets of dried seaweed)

kanpyo
(dried gourd ribbons)

kombu
(dried kelp for cooking rice)

white sesame seeds

black sesame seeds

renkon, sliced
(lotus root)

shiso leaf
(Japanese herb, also known as perilla)

Japanese ingredients are becoming more widely available in supermarkets and specialist food shops, but can certainly be found in Asian markets. This directory will help you identify them.

abura-age
(fried bean curd)

takuan
(pickled daikon radish)

fresh ginger

Japanese short-grained sushi rice

umeboshi
(pickled red plums)

ready-made pickled ginger

wasabi paste
(also available as powder in tins)

shiitake
(dried mushrooms, also available fresh)

Sushi is a general term for all food with 'sumeshi', or vinegared rice. Remember – sushi should never be put in the refrigerator (it will go hard). The vinegar will help preserve it for a few days if kept, wrapped, in a cool place, such as a shady window sill. To make sushi rice, boil 15 per cent more water than rice. So use 250 ml rice to 250 ml plus just over 1 tablespoon water.

vinegared rice sumeshi

400 ml Japanese rice*

1 piece of kombu
(dried kelp), 5 cm square,
for flavouring (optional)

3 tablespoons Japanese
rice vinegar

2½ tablespoons sugar

2 teaspoons sea salt

MAKES 1 LITRE

*Rice should always be measured
by volume, not weight.*

1 Put the rice in a large bowl and wash it thoroughly, changing the water several times, until the water is clear. Drain and leave in the strainer for 1 hour. If short of time, soak the rice in clear cold water for 10–15 minutes, then drain.

2 Transfer to a deep, heavy saucepan, add 460 ml water and a piece of kombu, if using. Cover and bring to the boil over high heat, about 5 minutes. Discard the kombu.

3 Lower the heat and simmer, covered, for about 10 minutes, or until all the water has been absorbed. Do not lift the lid until towards the end. Remove from the heat and leave, still covered, for about 10–15 minutes.

4 Mix the rice vinegar, sugar and salt in a small jug or bowl and stir until dissolved.

5 Transfer the cooked rice to a large, shallow dish or *handai* (Japanese wooden sumeshi tub). Sprinkle generously with the vinegar dressing.

6 Using a wooden spatula or spoon, fold the vinegar dressing into the rice. Do not stir. While folding, cool the rice quickly using a fan. Let the rice cool to body temperature before using to make sushi.

SUSHI ROLLS

Wonderful party food, nori rolls (*norimaki*) are probably the best-known sushi of all. A sheet of nori seaweed is spread with vinegared rice, a line of filling put down the middle, then the sheet is rolled up into a cylinder. The cylinder is cut into sections before serving. All ingredients are sold in Asian shops and larger supermarkets.

¾ recipe Vinegared Rice (page 11), divided into 3 portions

HAND VINEGAR
4 tablespoons Japanese rice vinegar
250 ml water

FOR ROLLING
18 cm piece of unwaxed cucumber, unpeeled
3 sheets nori seaweed
wasabi paste

TO SERVE
Pickled Ginger (page 123)
extra wasabi paste
Japanese soy sauce

a sushi rolling mat

MAKES 36 PIECES

simple rolled sushi norimaki

1 Mix the hand vinegar ingredients in a small bowl and set aside.

2 To prepare the cucumber, cut into quarters lengthways, then cut out the seeds and slice the remainder, lengthways, into 1 cm square matchstick strips. You need 6, each with some green skin.

3 Just before assembling, pass the nori over a very low gas flame or electric hotplate, just for a few seconds to make it crisp and bring out the flavour. Cut each sheet in half crossways.

4 Assemble the sushi according to the method on the following pages.

5 Cut each roll into 6 pieces.

6 Arrange on a platter and serve with pickled ginger, a little pile of wasabi and a dish of Japanese soy sauce.

making simple rolls step-by-step

Make the Vinegared Rice (page 11) and Hand Vinegar (page 13), then prepare and assemble the ingredients.

1 Put a sushi rolling mat on a work surface, then put ½ sheet of toasted nori seaweed on top. Take a handful of rice (2–3 heaped tablespoons) and make into a log shape. Put the rice in the middle of the nori.

2 Using your fingers, spread it evenly all over, leaving about 1.5 cm margin on the far side. (The rice will stick to your fingers, so dip them in the hand vinegar first.)

3 Take a small dot of wasabi paste on the end of your finger and draw a line down the middle across the rice, leaving a light green shadow on top of the rice (not too much – wasabi is very hot!)

4 Arrange 1 strip of cucumber across the rice, on top of the wasabi.

5 Pick up the mat from the near side and keep the cucumber in the centre.

6 Roll the mat over to meet the other side so that the rice stays inside the nori.

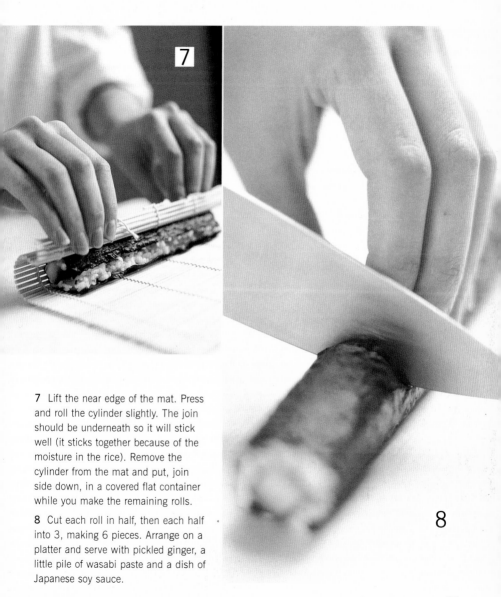

7 Lift the near edge of the mat. Press and roll the cylinder slightly. The join should be underneath so it will stick well (it sticks together because of the moisture in the rice). Remove the cylinder from the mat and put, join side down, in a covered flat container while you make the remaining rolls.

8 Cut each roll in half, then each half into 3, making 6 pieces. Arrange on a platter and serve with pickled ginger, a little pile of wasabi paste and a dish of Japanese soy sauce.

Other ingredients traditionally used for rolled sushi in Japan include *kanpyo* (dried gourd ribbons), tuna with spring onion, *natto* (steamed fermented soy beans), chilli-marinated cod's roe and *umeboshi* (salted plum) with shiso herb. You can also make variations using ingredients more readily available in the West.

rolled sushi variations

1 Mix the hand vinegar ingredients in a small bowl and set aside.

2 Cut the piece of salmon into 1 cm square strips. To make a salmon sushi, follow the method on pages 16–17, using a row of salmon strips instead of cucumber. (Enough to make 2 rolls.)

3 To make a pickled daikon sushi, follow the method on pages 16–17, using 3 strips of pickled daikon in a row instead of cucumber, and omitting the wasabi paste. (Enough to make 2 rolls.)

4 To make the pickled plum sushi, follow the method on pages 16–17, using the shiso or basil leaves and the pieces of plum. (Enough to make 2 rolls.)

5 Cut each roll into 6 pieces, then arrange on a plate and serve with pickled ginger, a mound of wasabi paste and a dish of soy sauce.

Note You can also leave the salmon fillet whole, then lightly grill it for about 2 minutes on each side. Cool, put in a bowl, flake with a fork, then stir in 2 finely chopped spring onions. Mix in salt, pepper and 2 teaspoons mayonnaise, then proceed as in the main recipe.

¾ recipe Vinegared Rice (page 11), divided into 3 portions

3 sheets nori seaweed

HAND VINEGAR

4 tablespoons Japanese rice vinegar

250 ml water

FILLINGS: YOUR CHOICE OF

100 g fresh salmon, skinned

6 cm pickled daikon (takuan), cut lengthways into 1 cm matchsticks

4–6 fresh shiso leaves or 6–8 basil leaves

2 small red pickled plums (umeboshi), pitted and torn into pieces

wasabi paste

TO SERVE

Pickled Ginger (page 123)

extra wasabi paste

Japanese soy sauce

a sushi rolling mat

MAKES 36 PIECES

big sushi rolls futomaki

3 sheets nori seaweed

1 recipe Vinegared Rice
(page 11), divided into
6 portions

HAND VINEGAR

4 tablespoons Japanese
rice vinegar

250 ml water

FILLINGS

9–12 uncooked king prawn
tails, unpeeled

1 recipe Japanese Omelette
(page 121)

250 g spinach

3 tablespoons Japanese
soy sauce

20 g dried gourd (kanpyo)
or 1 carrot, cut into
5 mm square shreds

5–6 dried shiitake mushrooms

2 tablespoons sugar

1 tablespoon mirin
(sweetened Japanese rice
wine) or sweet sherry

sea salt

TO SERVE

Japanese soy sauce

Pickled Ginger (page 123)

*8 cocktail sticks
or bamboo skewers*

a sushi rolling mat

MAKES 24 PIECES

1 Mix the hand vinegar ingredients in a small bowl and set aside.

2 Skewer a cocktail stick through each prawn from head to tail to prevent curling while cooking. Blanch in boiling water for 3 minutes until firm and pink. Immediately plunge into cold water and drain. Remove and discard the cocktail sticks, shells and dark back vein.

3 Cut the Japanese omelette lengthways into 1 cm square sticks.

4 Blanch the spinach in lightly salted water for 1 minute. Plunge into cold water. Drain and pat dry with kitchen paper. Sprinkle with 2 teaspoons soy sauce and set aside.

5 If using dried gourd, rub with salt and a little water, then soak in water for 10 minutes and drain. Cut into 20 cm lengths. Soak the shiitakes in warm water for 30 minutes, then drain, retaining the soaking water. Cut into 5 cm strips. Put 250 ml of the soaking liquid in a small saucepan with the remaining soy sauce, sugar and mirin. Bring to the boil. Add the gourd and shiitakes. Simmer over low heat for 15 minutes. Let cool in the liquid.

6 Toast the nori over a low gas flame or hotplate and put it crossways on a sushi rolling mat, following the method on page 15. Dip your hands in the hand vinegar. Take 1 portion of rice and squeeze it between your hands into a firm ball. Put the rice ball on one side of the nori sheet in the middle and, using wet fingers, spread it evenly over the half side of nori, leaving about 3 cm margin on the far side. Repeat this once more to fill the other half. The rice layer should be fairly thick – add extra rice if necessary.

7 Arrange 3–4 prawns in a row across the rice about 5 cm from the front edge. Add a row of omelette strips and a row of spinach on top of the prawns. Add a row of gourd or carrot and a row of shiitakes on top, so that all 5 ingredients are piled down the middle of the rice, like logs of wood. Each roll should use one-third of each ingredient.

8 Pick up the mat from the near side and roll the mat following the method on page 16. Remove the mat and put the roll on a plate, join side down. Repeat to make 2 more rolls. Cut each roll into 8 pieces and serve with soy sauce and pickled ginger.

children's favourites

Sushi is fun when you make it for or with children. Devising sushi for non-Japanese kids has led to some surprise discoveries.

1 Mix the hand vinegar ingredients in a bowl and set aside.

2 To make the fillings, strain the egg into a small bowl, add ½ tablespoon of the sugar and a pinch of salt and beat until dissolved. Heat a frying pan, brush with oil, then rub off any excess with kitchen paper.

3 Pour in the egg mixture and make a thin pancake, tilting the pan to spread it evenly. Prick any bubbles with a fork and fill any holes with egg by tilting the pan. After 30 seconds, turn the omelette over for 30 seconds to dry the other side and make it golden yellow. Remove from the heat, remove with a spatula and cut in half.

4 Blanch the carrot in about 250 ml boiling salted water for 2–3 minutes. Reduce the heat, then stir in the remaining 1½ tablespoons sugar and a pinch of salt. Simmer gently for 2–3 minutes, remove from the heat and let cool in the juice.

5 Put half the omelette on a board with the cut side nearest you and put a row of carrot strips beside the cut edge. Roll up the omelette tightly and secure the end with a cocktail stick. Repeat to make a second roll.

6 Cook the sausages according to the packet instructions and drain well on kitchen paper. Cut into 1 cm square matchsticks. Thickly peel the cucumber and finely shred the skin.

7 Put the canned salmon in a bowl, add the mayonnaise and pinch of salt and stir well.

8 Following the method on page 15, make 2 sushi rolls with a carrot-and-egg-roll filling (remove the cocktail sticks first), 2 rolls with strips of sausage and 2 with salmon paste and cucumber.

9 Cut each roll into 6 pieces and serve with soy sauce.

3 sheets nori seaweed

¾ recipe Vinegared Rice (page 11), divided into 6 portions

Japanese soy sauce, to serve

HAND VINEGAR

4 tablespoons Japanese rice vinegar

250 ml water

FILLINGS

1 egg, beaten

2 tablespoons sugar

6 cm carrot, sliced lengthways into 5 mm matchsticks

2 thin frankfurters, 18 cm long, or 4 Vienna sausages, 9 cm long

6 cm unwaxed cucumber

75 g canned red salmon, drained

1 tablespoon mayonnaise

sea salt

sunflower oil, for frying

a Japanese omelette pan or 20 cm non-stick frying pan

a sushi rolling mat

MAKES 36 PIECES

This is a very Western idea of sushi, but is easy and convenient because it uses canned tuna. Use Japanese mayonnaise if you can, but homemade or good-quality bought mayonnaise works well.

wasabi mayonnaise and tuna roll

4 sheets nori seaweed

185 g canned tuna in brine, drained

4 teaspoons Japanese or other mayonnaise

1 teaspoon wasabi paste, or to taste

125 g baby corn, fresh or frozen, or equivalent canned baby corn, drained

½ recipe Vinegared Rice (page 11), divided into 4 portions

HAND VINEGAR

4 tablespoons Japanese rice vinegar

250 ml water

a sushi rolling mat

MAKES 24–28 PIECES

1 Mix the hand vinegar ingredients in a small bowl and set aside.

2 Trim a 2.5 cm strip from one long edge of each sheet of nori and reserve for another use.

3 Put the tuna and mayonnaise in a bowl and stir in the wasabi.

4 If using fresh or frozen corn, bring a saucepan of water to the boil and cook the corn for 3 minutes or until tender. Drain and rinse under cold water to cool. If using canned corn, drain and rinse.

5 Put a sheet of nori, rough side up with the long edge towards you, on a sushi rolling mat. Dip your fingers in the hand vinegar, and top the nori with 1 portion of vinegared rice, then spread it in a thin layer, leaving about 2 cm of bare nori on the far edge. Spoon 1 portion of the tuna mixture in a line along the middle of the rice and top with a line of baby corn, set end to end.

6 Lift the near edge of the mat and start rolling the sushi away from you, pressing in the filling with your fingers as you roll. You may need a little water along the far edge to seal it. Repeat to make 4 rolls.

7 Using a clean, wet knife, slice each roll into 6–7 even pieces.

Fresh tuna is one of the most popular fillings for sushi. There are three main cuts, the pink *otoro* (the finest), *chutoro* and the dark red *akami*. With their incredible popularity and high price tags, otoro and chutoro are delicacies reserved for sashimi, but the akami is perfect for rolled sushi.

spicy tuna roll

1 Mix the hand vinegar ingredients in a small bowl and set aside.

2 Slice the tuna into 1 cm strips and put in a shallow dish. Mix the soy sauce, sake, hot pepper sauce and spring onions in a bowl. Pour over the tuna and stir well to coat. Cover and let marinate for 30 minutes. Divide into 6 portions.

3 Put ½ sheet of nori, rough side up with the long edge towards you, on a sushi rolling mat. Dip your fingers in the hand vinegar, then top the nori with 1 portion of vinegared rice and spread in a thin layer, leaving about 2 cm of bare nori on the far edge. Set 1 portion of the tuna strips in a line along the middle of the rice.

4 Lift the near edge of the mat and start rolling the sushi away from you, pressing in the filling with your fingers as you roll. You may need a little water along the far edge to seal it. Repeat to make 6 rolls.

5 Using a clean wet knife, slice each roll into 6–7 even pieces.

300 g fresh tuna

2 tablespoons Japanese soy sauce

1 tablespoon sake

1 teaspoon Chinese hot pepper sauce, or chilli sauce

2 spring onions, finely chopped

3 sheets nori seaweed, halved

½ recipe Vinegared Rice (page 11), divided into 6 portions

HAND VINEGAR

4 tablespoons Japanese rice vinegar

250 ml water

a sushi rolling mat

MAKES 36–42 PIECES

Soaking in vinegar is a way of mellowing the strong flavours of some fish, such as mackerel. If you don't have time to prepare fresh mackerel, try making this sushi with smoked mackerel or other smoked fish for a different, but still delicious flavour.

vinegared mackerel and avocado roll

400 g fresh mackerel fillets (about 2 medium fillets)

2 tablespoons sea salt

5 tablespoons rice vinegar

1 tablespoon sugar

1 avocado

3 sheets nori seaweed, halved

½ recipe Vinegared Rice (page 11), divided into 6 portions

1 teaspoon wasabi paste (optional)

HAND VINEGAR

4 tablespoons Japanese rice vinegar

250 ml water

a sushi rolling mat

MAKES 36–42 PIECES

1 Mix the hand vinegar ingredients in a small bowl and set aside.

2 Put the mackerel fillets in a shallow, non-metal bowl and sprinkle on both sides with the salt. Cover with clingfilm and refrigerate for 8 hours or overnight.

3 Remove the fish from the refrigerator, rinse under cold running water and pat dry with kitchen paper. Put the vinegar and sugar in a shallow dish, mix well, then add the mackerel, turning to coat. Let marinate for 40 minutes at room temperature.

4 Remove the fish from the marinade and slice diagonally into 1 cm strips. Slice the avocado into 1 cm strips.

5 Put a sheet of nori, rough side up with the long edge towards you, on a sushi rolling mat. Dip your fingers in the hand vinegar, take 1 portion of the vinegared rice and spread it out in a thin layer, leaving about 2 cm bare on the far edge. Smear a little wasabi, if using, down the middle of the rice. Arrange a line of mackerel slices over the wasabi and top with a line of the avocado.

6 Lift the near edge of the mat and start rolling the sushi away from you, pressing in the filling with your fingers as you roll. You may need a little water along the far edge to seal it. Repeat with the remaining ingredients to make 6 rolls. Using a clean, wet knife, slice each roll into 6–7 even pieces.

A fresh oyster makes such an elegantly simple topping for sushi. Chose small oysters if possible – large ones will swamp a delicate roll.

fresh oyster roll
with chilli cucumber

2 sheets nori seaweed

½ recipe Vinegared Rice (page 11), divided into 2 portions

freshly squeezed juice of 1 lemon

20 small raw oysters, shucked

CHILLI CUCUMBER

125 ml white rice vinegar

2 tablespoons sugar

1 tablespoon mirin (sweetened Japanese rice wine)

7 cm piece cucumber, halved, deseeded and cut into fine matchsticks

2 mild red chillies, halved, deseeded and finely sliced

HAND VINEGAR

4 tablespoons Japanese rice vinegar

250 ml water

a sushi rolling mat

MAKES 20 PIECES

1 To make the chilli cucumber, put the vinegar, sugar and mirin in a small saucepan and bring to the boil, stirring. Reduce the heat and simmer for 3 minutes. Remove from the heat and let cool.

2 Put the cucumber and chillies in a plastic bowl and pour over the cooled vinegar mixture. Cover and refrigerate for 24 hours.

3 When ready to assemble the rolls, mix the hand vinegar ingredients in a small bowl and set aside.

4 Put a sheet of nori, rough side up with the long edge towards you, on a sushi rolling mat. Dip your fingers in the hand vinegar, take 1 portion of the vinegared rice and spread it out in a thin layer, leaving about 2 cm bare on the far edge. Lift the edge of the mat closest to you and start rolling the sushi away from you. You may need a little water along the far edge to seal it. Press the roll into an oval. Repeat with the remaining ingredients to make a second roll.

5 Using a clean, wet knife, slice each roll in half, then each half into 5 even pieces, making 20.

6 Sprinkle lemon juice over the oysters. Top each piece of sushi with an oyster and a little chilli cucumber.

Uramaki is an 'inside-out' roll, with nori inside and rice outside. This prawn tempura version is popular in restaurants – the nori prevents the vinegar in the rice and the oil in the tempura from touching each other.

inside-out sushi uramaki

2 sheets nori seaweed

¾ recipe Vinegared Rice (page 11), divided into 4 portions

HAND VINEGAR

2 tablespoons Japanese rice vinegar

125 ml water

TEMPURA PRAWNS

8 large uncooked tiger prawns, 4 peeled completely, 4 left with tail fins intact, deveined

100 g plain flour, sifted

4 tablespoons sesame seeds, black or white

sea salt

sunflower oil, for frying

TO SERVE

Pickled Ginger (page 123)

Japanese soy sauce

8 cocktail sticks or bamboo skewers

a sushi rolling mat

MAKES 20 PIECES

1 Mix the hand vinegar ingredients in a small bowl. Skewer a cocktail stick through each prawn from top to tail to prevent curling while cooking.

2 Cover one side of a sushi rolling mat with clingfilm and put it on a dry cutting board, clingfilm side up.

3 Fill a wok or deep saucepan one-third full of oil and heat to 170°C (340°F) or until a cube of bread browns in 60 seconds. To make the tempura batter, put 100 ml water in a bowl, sift the flour into the water and mix with a fork. One by one, dip the prawns in the batter, then fry in the hot oil for 3–4 minutes or until golden brown. Remove and drain on kitchen paper and carefully remove and discard the cocktail sticks.

4 Put the nori on a completely dry cutting board. Dip your hands in the hand vinegar. Take a handful of the rice (2–3 heaped tablespoons) in your hands and make into a log shape. Put the rice in the centre of the nori. Using your fingers, spread it evenly all over, right to the edges. Sprinkle 1 tablespoon sesame seeds all over the rice.

5 Turn the whole thing over onto the clingfilm-covered mat.

6 Arrange 2 tempura prawns down the centre of the nori, with the tails sticking out at the ends (remove the tail fins if you like).

7 Roll the mat following the method on pages 16–17. Remove from the mat and repeat to make 3 more rolls.

8 Cut each roll into 5 pieces and arrange on a platter. Serve with pickled ginger and a little soy sauce in a small dish beside the platter or in small individual plates.

slow-cooked squid sushi

Squid is delicious in sushi, but can be tricky when raw, because it does tend to be tough. If you braise it slowly, you end up with deliciously tender pieces.

250 g baby squid tubes, 8 cm long (about 12), cleaned

1 teaspoon mirin (sweetened Japanese rice wine)

1 teaspoon soy sauce

½ teaspoon finely chopped fresh red chilli

½ teaspoon finely chopped garlic

1 teaspoon grated fresh ginger

1 tablespoon finely chopped fresh coriander

½ recipe Vinegared Rice (page 11)

1 tablespoon black sesame seeds

HAND VINEGAR

4 tablespoons Japanese rice vinegar

250 ml water

an oven tray or grill tray

MAKES 24 PIECES

1 Slice the squid tubes in half lengthways and arrange on an oven tray or grill tray. Sprinkle with the mirin and soy. Set the tray at least 15 cm away from a preheated grill so the heat is not too fierce. Grill for about 8 minutes or until the squid turns opaque. Remove and let cool.

2 Put the squid in a bowl, add the chilli, garlic, ginger and coriander, stir gently, cover and marinate in the refrigerator for 1 hour.

3 Mix the hand vinegar ingredients in a small bowl and set aside.

4 Dip your fingers in the hand vinegar and divide the rice into 24 walnut-sized balls.

5 Top each rice ball with a piece of squid using the natural curl of the squid body to hold it securely. Sprinkle with a few black sesame seeds, then serve.

yakitori octopus roll

Yakitori is the name given to food grilled on skewers over charcoal. It can be anything – chicken, steak, liver, or the octopus used here. Prawns, scallops or any firm fish also work well.

1 Cut the octopus into 2 cm pieces. Cut the spring onions into 2 cm lengths. Thread the pieces of octopus and spring onion alternately crossways onto the soaked skewers.

2 Put the sake, soy, sugar and ginger into a small bowl or jug, mix well, then pour over the octopus skewers and let marinate at room temperature for 30 minutes, turning occasionally.

3 Preheat a barbecue or grill to very hot. Set the yakitori skewers about 7 cm from the heat and cook for 4–5 minutes, turning once. Remove from the heat and let cool.

4 Mix the hand vinegar ingredients in a small bowl and set aside.

5 Put a sheet of nori, rough side up with the long edge towards you, on a sushi rolling mat. Dip your fingers in the hand vinegar and add 1 portion of the vinegared rice, spread in a thin layer, leaving about 2 cm of bare nori on the far edge. Arrange pieces of the octopus, end to end, in a line along the middle of the rice, then put a line of spring onions on top.

6 Lift the edge of the mat closest to you and start rolling the sushi away from you, pressing in the filling with your fingers as you roll. You may need a little water along the far edge to seal it. Repeat to make 6 rolls.

7 Using a clean wet knife, slice each roll into 5 even pieces.

Note If the octopus has not been pre-tenderized, you can either beat it with a meat mallet or try this Portuguese method. Put in a large saucepan with 1 sliced onion. Cover with a lid and slowly bring to the boil over low heat (there will be enough moisture in the octopus to do this without added water). Let simmer for 30–40 minutes until tender. Cool, then pull off and discard the purple skin and suckers.

6 octopus tentacles, about 1 kg, tenderized, skin and suckers removed

6 spring onions

2 tablespoons sake

2 tablespoons Japanese soy sauce

1 teaspoon sugar

1 teaspoon freshly grated ginger

3 sheets nori seaweed, halved

½ recipe Vinegared Rice (page 11), divided into 6 portions

HAND VINEGAR

4 tablespoons Japanese rice vinegar

250 ml water

5 bamboo skewers, soaked in water for 30 minutes

a sushi rolling mat

MAKES 30 PIECES

To many sushi fans, delicious raw fish is part of the pleasure of this dish. However, if you're not an aficionado of fish *au naturel*, using smoked or pickled fish is a delicious compromise. It is very easy to pickle fish at home, and you can control the sharpness more easily.

pickled salmon roll

1 To prepare the salmon, put the vinegar, salt, sugar and lemon zest in a saucepan with 60 ml water. Bring to the boil, reduce the heat, then simmer for 3 minutes. Let cool.

2 Put the salmon fillet in a plastic container with the shallots. Pour the vinegar mixture over the top and cover tightly. Refrigerate for 2–3 days, turning the salmon in the pickle once a day.

3 When ready to make the sushi, drain the salmon and shallots. Slice the salmon as finely as possible and divide into 6 portions.

4 Mix the hand vinegar ingredients in a small bowl and set aside.

5 Put a piece of nori, rough side up with the long edge towards you, on a sushi rolling mat. Dip your fingers in the hand vinegar, then take 1 portion of the vinegared rice and spread it out in a thin layer, leaving about 2 cm of bare nori at the far edge. Smear a little wasabi down the centre of the rice if you like. Arrange 1 portion of the salmon slices in a line along the middle of the rice and top with a line of the pickled shallots.

6 Lift the near edge of the mat and start rolling the sushi away from you, pressing in the filling with your fingers as you roll. You may need a little water along the far edge to seal it. Repeat with the remaining ingredients to make 6 rolls.

7 Using a clean wet knife, slice each roll into 6–7 even pieces, then serve.

3 sheets nori seaweed, halved

½ recipe Vinegared Rice (page 11), divided into 6 portions

1 teaspoon wasabi paste (optional)

PICKLED SALMON

100 ml rice wine vinegar

2 teaspoons sea salt

2 tablespoons sugar

zest of 1 unwaxed lemon, removed with a lemon zester

300 g salmon fillet, skinned and boned

4 shallots, finely sliced

HAND VINEGAR

4 tablespoons Japanese rice vinegar

250 ml water

a sushi rolling mat

MAKES 36–42 PIECES

tempura prawn roll

The crunch of tempura batter is delicious in sushi, although the batter will soften as it cools. If you have some left over, use it to cook vegetables or for the tempura croutons for miso soup on page 117.

24 large uncooked prawns, peeled, but with tail fins intact

2 sheets nori seaweed

½ recipe Vinegared Rice (page 11)

1 teaspoon wasabi (optional)

25 g mizuna or baby spinach

peanut or sunflower oil, for frying

TEMPURA BATTER

1 egg, separated

1 tablespoon freshly squeezed lemon juice

150 ml iced water

60 g plain flour

HAND VINEGAR

4 tablespoons Japanese rice vinegar

250 ml water

24 bamboo skewers

MAKES 24 PIECES

1 Fill a large wok or saucepan one-third full with oil and heat to 190°C (375°F), or until a small cube of bread turns golden in 30 seconds.

2 Thread each prawn onto a skewer to straighten it for cooking.

3 To make the batter, put the egg yolk, lemon juice and iced water in a bowl. Whisk gently, then whisk in the flour to form a smooth batter. Do not overmix.

4 Whisk the egg white in a second bowl until stiff but not dry, then fold into the batter.

5 Dip each prawn into the batter and fry for 1–2 minutes until crisp and golden. Drain on crumpled kitchen paper and let cool for 5 minutes. Remove the skewers.

6 Mix the hand vinegar ingredients in a small bowl and set aside.

7 Using dry hands, cut the nori sheets in half crossways and then into 3 cm strips. Spread 1 tablespoon of rice over each piece of nori, top with a tempura prawn, a dab of wasabi, if using, and a little mizuna or baby spinach. Roll up to secure the filling. Brush the nori with water to help it stick, if necessary. Repeat until all the ingredients have been used.

This battleship-shaped version of nigiri-zushi (page 49) has a ribbon of nori seaweed wrapped vertically around the rice, with added toppings such as salmon caviar (*ikura* or keta) and sea urchin. This recipe includes Western variations using crabmeat.

battleship rolls
gunkanmaki

1½ sheets nori seaweed

½ recipe Vinegared Rice (page 11)

HAND VINEGAR

4 tablespoons Japanese rice vinegar

250 ml water

TOPPINGS

8–12 tablespoons crabmeat*

about 1 teaspoon sake

2 teaspoons wasabi paste or powder

4–6 tablespoons salmon caviar (ikura or keta) or red lumpfish caviar

12 pickled caperberries or capers

TO SERVE

Pickled Ginger (page 123), to serve

Japanese soy sauce

MAKES 12 PIECES

Use white and brown crabmeat from your fishmonger, or good-quality canned crab.

1 Mix the hand vinegar ingredients in a small bowl and set aside.

2 Put the crabmeat on a small plate and sprinkle with a little sake. If using wasabi powder, mix 1–2 teaspoons powder in an egg cup with 1–2 teaspoons water to make a clay-like consistency. Turn it upside down and set aside to prevent it drying.

3 Cut the whole sheet of nori crossways into 8 ribbons, 18 x 2.5 cm, and the ½ sheet into 4, making 12 ribbons in total.

4 Dip your hands in the hand vinegar, then take 1–2 tablespoons rice in one hand and squeeze it into a rectangular mound about 5 x 2 x 3 cm high. Wrap a nori ribbon around it, overlapping about 2 cm at the end. Glue it together with a grain of vinegared rice. Put 2 teaspoons caviar and a few pickled caperberries or capers on top. Repeat to make 3 more rolls with caviar, 4 with crabmeat topped with a little salmon caviar and 4 with crabmeat, with a tiny dot of wasabi on top.

5 Arrange on a platter, then serve with the pickled ginger and a small dish of soy sauce as party food. If making individual servings, serve the soy sauce in small, separate dishes.

Battleship sushi is individually hand rolled so the nori comes about half a centimetre above the rice, leaving room for less manageable toppings such as fish roe. Small cubes of differently coloured fish make a lovely topping and you don't need to be an expert fish slicer to get tender pieces. You do, however, need very fresh raw fish – that is what 'sushi- or sashimi-grade' means. If you have access to a proper Japanese fishmonger, that's perfect. Otherwise, go to a fish market, or other outlet, where you can be sure the fish is ultra-fresh.

75 g piece of sashimi-grade
raw salmon

75 g piece of sashimi-grade
raw tuna

75 g piece of sashimi-grade
raw white fish
(try sea bream or halibut)

½ recipe Vinegared Rice
(page 11)

4 sheets nori seaweed

1 teaspoon wasabi paste
(optional)

1 tablespoon salmon caviar
(ikura or keta)

HAND VINEGAR

4 tablespoons Japanese
rice vinegar

250 ml water

MAKES 18 PIECES

treasures of the sea battleship sushi

1 Cut the salmon, tuna and white fish into ½ cm cubes, put in a bowl and mix gently.

2 Mix the hand vinegar ingredients in a small bowl.

3 Dip your fingers in the hand vinegar and divide the vinegared rice into 18 portions, a little smaller than a table tennis ball. Gently squeeze each piece into a flattened oval shape, about 2 cm high. With dry hands, cut the nori sheets into 2.5 cm strips, then wrap each piece of rice in one strip with the rough side of the nori facing inwards. Seal the ends with a dab of water. You should have about ½ cm of nori above the rice.

4 Put a dab of wasabi, if using, on top of the rice, then add a heaped teaspoon of the fish cubes and a little salmon caviar.

Battleship rolls can be made with lettuce leaves instead of nori. Use iceberg to make cups and a lettuce with flexible leaves, such as butter lettuce or lollo rosso, to make ribbons.

lettuce rolls

1 Mix the hand vinegar ingredients in a small bowl and set aside.

2 Put the haddock and bay leaf in a saucepan, cover with boiling water, return to the boil, then simmer for 5 minutes or until cooked. Drain well. Remove and discard the skin and all the small bones. Put in a bowl and flake finely with a fork. Stir in the sugar and let cool.

3 Sprinkle the smoked salmon with lemon juice.

4 Cut 3 cm strips crossways from the outside edges of the lollo rosso and butter lettuce leaves. Make small cups, 7 cm diameter, from the inner iceberg leaves.

5 Make 12 rectangular mounds of rice, following the method on page 43. Instead of wrapping in nori, wrap 4 in lollo rosso leaves, 4 in butter lettuce and 4 in iceberg lettuce cups. Put about 1 tablespoon of haddock flakes on top of the rice in the lollo rosso leaves. Put about 1 tablespoon smoked salmon on the rice in the butter lettuce and about 1 tablespoon caviar in the iceberg cups. Top the haddock with a little caviar, the salmon with a caperberry or caper and the caviar with a few flakes of haddock.

6 Arrange on a platter or small plates and serve with a small dish of soy sauce.

4 small lollo rosso or oakleaf lettuce leaves

4 butter lettuce leaves

4 small iceberg lettuce leaves

½ recipe Vinegared Rice (page 11)

Japanese soy sauce, to serve

HAND VINEGAR

4 tablespoons Japanese rice vinegar

250 ml water

TOPPINGS

75 g smoked haddock

1 bay leaf

1 teaspoon sugar

75 g smoked salmon, finely chopped

1 tablespoon lemon juice

4–6 tablespoons black lumpfish caviar

1 tablespoon caperberries or capers, drained

MAKES 12 PIECES

hand-moulded sushi nigiri-zushi

Nigiri is the king of all sushi. Though it looks simple, it is actually the most difficult to make and is not usually made at home, even in Japan.

1 Mix the hand vinegar ingredients in a small bowl and set aside.

2 Push a bamboo skewer through each prawn from top to tail to prevent curling while cooking. Blanch in boiling water for 2 minutes until lightly cooked and pink. Drain and cool under running water. Drain and discard the cocktail sticks, shells and back vein. Make a slit up the belly and open out.

3 Slice the tuna or salmon and sea bream into rectangular pieces, 7 x 3 x 1 cm thick. Cut the squid into similar rectangular pieces, and make fine slits on one side of each piece to make the squid more tender.

4 Using the beaten eggs, dashi, mirin and soy sauce, make an omelette following the method on page 121. Put the rolled omelette on a sushi mat and tightly roll into a flat rectangular shape. When cool, cut 2 rectangular pieces, 7 x 3 x 1 cm thick.

5 If using wasabi powder, mix with 2 teaspoons water in an egg cup and stir well to make a clay-like consistency. Leave upside down to prevent drying.

6 Dip your hands in the hand vinegar mixture, take 1–2 tablespoons of the cooked rice in one hand and mould into a rectangular cylinder about 5 x 2 x 2 cm. Put a tiny bit of wasabi on top and cover with an opened prawn.

7 Repeat, making 2 nigiri topped with prawns, 2 with tuna or salmon, 2 with sea bream, 2 with squid on top of a shiso leaf and 2 with omelette. When assembling the nigiri with omelette, do not add wasabi: instead, tie with a thin nori ribbon, about 5 mm wide.

8 Arrange on a platter and serve with pickled ginger and Japanese soy sauce in a small dish. Alternatively, serve as party canapés or on small plates as part of a meal.

⅓ recipe Vinegared Rice (page 11)

HAND VINEGAR

4 tablespoons Japanese rice vinegar

250 ml water

JAPANESE OMELETTE

2 eggs, beaten

2 tablespoons Dashi (page 109)

1 teaspoon mirin (sweetened Japanese rice wine) or sweet sherry

1 teaspoon Japanese soy sauce

TOPPINGS

2 uncooked tiger prawn tails

1 fillet fresh tuna or salmon, about 100 g, skinned

1 fillet fresh sea bream, about 100 g, skinned

100 g squid, cleaned and skinned

2 teaspoons wasabi paste or powder

2 shiso leaves or basil leaves

a small piece of nori seaweed, cut into 5 mm strips

sea salt

TO SERVE

Pickled Ginger (page 123), to serve

Japanese soy sauce

2 bamboo skewers

a sushi rolling mat

MAKES 8–10 PIECES

An alternative way to serve the nigiri from page 49 is in lettuce 'boats'. They look very pretty and are also easier to pick up and eat – important at a party.

lettuce boats

½ recipe Vinegared Rice (page 11)

HAND VINEGAR

4 tablespoons Japanese rice vinegar

250 ml water

TOPPINGS

100 g tender beef fillet, about 7 cm thick

vegetable oil, for rubbing

iced water

1–2 rollmops (marinated Bismarck herring)

8 asparagus tips

2 teaspoons wasabi paste

4 Little Gem lettuce leaves

8 small chicory (witloof) leaves

TO SERVE

sprigs of cress or shredded spring onions

a small strip of nori seaweed

1 spring onion, finely chopped

2.5 cm fresh ginger, peeled and grated

2 tablespoons white wine

1½ tablespoons Japanese soy sauce, plus extra for serving

freshly squeezed juice of ½ lemon

MAKES 12 PIECES

1 Mix the hand vinegar ingredients in a small bowl and set aside.

2 Rub the beef all over with vegetable oil. Grill at a high heat until golden brown on all sides, but rare in the middle. Plunge into iced water to stop the cooking. Remove from the water, pat dry with kitchen paper and cut 4 thin slices, about 7 x 4 cm. All the slices should be red inside and brown around the edges.

3 Cut the rollmops into 4 and make a little lengthways slit in the skin of each piece.

4 Cook the asparagus in lightly salted water for 5 minutes until soft. Drain and cool under running water to arrest cooking and bring out the colour. Pat dry with kitchen paper.

5 Dip your hands in the hand vinegar and take 1–2 tablespoons of the cooked rice in one hand. Mould it into a rectangular shape about 5 x 2 x 2 cm. Repeat with the remaining rice, making 12 portions. Put a tiny dab of wasabi on top of 4 portions.

6 Arrange a slice of beef on 1 portion of wasabi and rice, with the 2 short sides hanging over the end. Top with a few sprigs of cress. Repeat with the other 3 slices of beef and set them in Little Gem lettuce leaves.

7 Arrange 2 asparagus tips on another rice portion and tie with a nori ribbon. Repeat to make 3 more. Arrange a piece of rollmop on each of the remaining 4 rice portions and insert chopped spring onion and grated ginger into the slits. Arrange all the leaf boats on a serving platter. To make a lemon sauce, mix the white wine, soy sauce and lemon juice in a small bowl. Serve the lettuce boats with a small bowl of lemon sauce and another of plain soy sauce.

teriyaki chicken roll
with miso dipping sauce

1 Mix the hand vinegar ingredients in a small bowl and set aside.

2 To make the teriyaki sauce, mix the soy, mirin and stock in a saucepan and bring to the boil. Remove from the heat and let cool.

3 To make the teriyaki glaze, mix the sugar and cornflour in a small bowl with a little cold water to slacken, then stir in 2 tablespoons of the teriyaki sauce. Set aside.

4 Thread the strips of chicken onto the soaked skewers. Brush the skewers with half the teriyaki sauce and let marinate for about 10 minutes. Preheat a grill or barbecue to very hot. Set the chicken skewers under or over the grill and cook for 2–3 minutes. Turn the skewers over, brush with more sauce and grill for 2–3 minutes until cooked. Remove from the heat, pour over the teriyaki glaze, let cool, then unthread. The chicken must be cold.

5 Set a sheet of nori, rough side up with the long edge towards you, on a sushi rolling mat. Dip your fingers in the hand vinegar and put quarter of the vinegared rice on the nori and spread in a thin layer covering about half of the nori closest to you. Put a quarter of the chicken in a line along the middle of the rice and smear with a little wasabi.

6 Lift the near edge of the mat and start rolling the sushi away from you, pressing in the filling with your fingers as you roll. You may need a little water along the far edge to seal it. Repeat with the remaining ingredients to make 4 rolls. Using a clean, wet knife, slice each roll into 6–7 even pieces.

7 To make the white miso dipping sauce, put the miso, sugar and sake in a small saucepan over medium heat and bring to a simmer, reduce the heat to low and cook for 3 minutes, stirring constantly to stop it burning.

8 Remove from the heat and quickly stir in the egg yolk, strain if necessary, and let cool before serving with the sushi.

400 g boneless, skinless chicken thigh or breast (2 breasts, 4 thighs), cut into 1 cm strips

4 sheets of nori

½ recipe Vinegared Rice (page 11), divided into 4 portions

1 teaspoon wasabi paste

HAND VINEGAR

4 tablespoons Japanese rice vinegar

250 ml water

TERIYAKI SAUCE

2 tablespoons Japanese soy sauce

2 tablespoons mirin (sweetened Japanese rice wine)

2 tablespoons chicken stock

TERIYAKI GLAZE

1 teaspoon sugar

½ teaspoon cornflour

MISO DIPPING SAUCE

2 tablespoons white miso paste

1 tablespoon sugar

125 ml sake

1 small egg yolk, beaten

12 bamboo skewers soaked in water for 30 minutes

a sushi rolling mat

MAKES 24–28 PIECES

Pickled plums (*umeboshi*) can be bought in Japanese and Asian supermarkets. They can be very salty and sharp, so you don't need much. If you do not like the flavour of pickled plum, replace with pickled ginger.

sushi balls with roast pork and pickled plums

250 g pork fillet, in the piece

2 tablespoons Japanese soy sauce

1 tablespoon mirin (sweetened Japanese rice wine)

1 teaspoon Chinese hot pepper sauce or chilli sauce

½ recipe Vinegared Rice (page 11)

10 Japanese pickled plums, halved and stoned

a roasting tin

MAKES 20 PIECES

1 Put the pork in a plastic container. Mix the soy, mirin and hot pepper sauce in a bowl or jug, then pour over the pork. Set aside to marinate for 1 hour, turning the pork in the marinade every 15 minutes.

2 Put the pork in a roasting tin and pour the marinade over the top. Roast in a preheated oven at 200°C (400°F) Gas 6 for 15 minutes. Remove from the oven, let cool, then slice thinly – you should get about 20 slices.

3 Divide the rice into 20 balls. Take a piece of pickled plum and push it into the centre of a rice ball, then mould the rice around it so it is completely hidden. Repeat with the remaining plums and rice. Top each ball with a slice of roast pork.

marinated beef sushi
beef tataki

Beef tataki is very rare marinated beef served in the sashimi style. If you do not like very rare beef, cook the fillet in a preheated oven at 180 °C (350 °F) Gas 4 for 10 minutes before returning to the frying pan to coat with sauce.

2 teaspoons peanut oil

300 g beef eye fillet, in the piece

2 tablespoons Japanese soy sauce

2 tablespoons mirin (sweetened Japanese rice wine)

2 tablespoons Japanese rice vinegar

½ recipe Vinegared Rice (page 11)

shredded Pickled Ginger (page 123), to serve (optional)

PICKLED RED CABBAGE

175 g (about ⅛) red cabbage

100 g brown sugar

125 ml red wine vinegar

MAKES 18 SUSHI PIECES, 250 ML PICKLED CABBAGE

1 To make the pickled red cabbage, finely slice the cabbage, removing any large core pieces, and chop the slices into 3 cm lengths. Put in a medium saucepan, then add the brown sugar, vinegar and 4 tablespoons water. Bring to the boil, reduce the heat and simmer for 30 minutes.

2 Remove from the heat, let cool and store in a sealed container in the refrigerator for up to 1 week, or in the freezer for 3 months.

3 To prepare the beef, heat the oil in a frying pan and sear the beef on all sides until browned. Mix the soy sauce, mirin and vinegar in a bowl and pour over the beef, turning to coat. Remove immediately from the heat and transfer the meat and its sauce to a dish. Let cool, cover and refrigerate for 1 hour, turning once.

4 Divide the rice into 18 walnut-sized balls, then shape into firm ovals.

5 Cut the beef in half lengthways (along the natural separation line), then slice as finely as possible. Wrap a piece of beef around the top of a rice ball and top with a little pickled cabbage or ginger.

A perfect sushi for parties. Serve the rice, nori sheets and prepared ingredients on plates and let people roll their own. Choose ingredients with varied tastes and colours. This is a delicious variation of the hand roll using smoked salmon instead of crabsticks.

smoked salmon hand rolls temaki

4 sheets nori seaweed
or 8 salad leaves

¾ recipe Vinegared Rice
(page 11)

Pickled Ginger (page 123),
to serve

HAND ROLL FILLINGS

125 g smoked salmon

4 spring onions

6 cm pickled daikon (takuan)

1 avocado

freshly squeezed juice
of 1 lemon

MAKES 8 ROLLS

1 Cut the smoked salmon lengthways into 5 mm wide strips.

2 Finely slice the spring onions lengthways into 8–10 cm strips. Slice the pickled daikon thinly.

3 Cut the avocado in half, remove the stone and peel carefully. Thinly slice the flesh and brush with lemon juice.

4 Toast the nori sheets by quickly passing over a low flame or a hotplate to make them crisp and bring out the flavour. Cut each sheet in half crossways.

5 Put the rice in a serving bowl and arrange the salmon, spring onion and avocado on a platter. Serve them with the nori and pickled ginger on small separate plates.

6 To assemble, follow the step-by-step directions on the following page.

assembling hand rolls step-by-step

1 Take one piece of nori seaweed in one hand and add 2–3 tablespoons of vinegared rice. Spread the rice over half the nori.

2 Arrange your choice of fillings diagonally over the rice from the centre to the outer corner.

3 Take the bottom right-hand corner and curl it towards the middle to form a cone.

4 Keep rolling the cone until complete. To glue the cone closed (optional), put a few grains of rice on the edge of the nori, and press together.

5 When the cone is complete, add your choice of a few drops of soy sauce, a few pieces of pickled ginger and a dab of wasabi paste.

california rolls

Oboro are fine white fish flakes, usually coloured pink, making them perfect for adding a splash of colour to sushi. These tiny hand rolls are very easy to eat with your fingers, and so make perfect party food. If you mix all the ingredients before rolling the sushi, the process will be a lot easier.

7 cm piece of cucumber

150 g crabmeat

1 small or ½ medium (firm) avocado, cut into small cubes

½ recipe Vinegared Rice (page 11)

6–7 sheets of nori

1 teaspoon wasabi paste (optional)

1 tablespoon oboro (optional, see recipe introduction)

MAKES 60–70 ROLLS

1 Slice the cucumber in half lengthways and scrape out the seeds. Chop the flesh into tiny cubes and put in a bowl. Add the crabmeat, avocado and rice and mix gently.

2 Cut each sheet of nori in half lengthways, then cut the halves into 5 pieces crossways (9 x 4 cm).

3 Put 1 piece of nori, rough side up with the long edge towards you, on a work surface. Spread 1 teaspoon of the rice mixture crossways over the nori about quarter of the way in from the left edge. Smear the rice with a little wasabi, if using. Take the bottom left corner of the nori and fold it diagonally so the left edge meets the top edge, then continue folding the whole triangle. Sprinkle the open end with a little oboro, if using. Repeat until all the ingredients have been used.

This larger hand roll is still small enough to be held and eaten easily, but also makes a great starter or lunch if you allow 3 rolls per person. Choose any smoked fish, but make sure it is moist and soft.

smoked fish hand roll

1 Put the onion in a small saucepan with the vinegar and 4 tablespoons water. Bring to the boil, drain and let cool.

2 Cut the smoked fish into even strips, about 6 x 1 cm long – you should have 18 even pieces.

3 Quarter the cucumber lengthways, scrape out the seeds, then cut into fine strips.

4 Cut each sheet of nori into 3 pieces (18 x 7 cm).

5 Put a piece of nori, rough side up with the long edge towards you. Spread 1 small heaped teaspoon of rice crossways over the nori about a quarter of the way in from the left edge. Smear with a little wasabi, if using. Top the rice with a piece of fish, a few strips of carrot, red pepper and cucumber and a little red onion, pressing slightly into the rice to hold it firm while you roll.

6 Take the bottom left corner of the nori and fold it diagonally so the left edge meets the top edge. Continue folding the whole triangle. Arrange with the join downwards on a serving plate or tray. Repeat to make 18 rolls altogether.

7 Serve with soy sauce.

1 small red onion, finely sliced

1 tablespoon rice vinegar

180 g smoked fish, such as trout, salmon or eel

5 cm piece of cucumber

6 sheets of nori, about 21 x 18 cm

½ recipe Vinegared Rice (page 11)

1 teaspoon wasabi paste (optional)

1 small carrot, finely sliced into thin strips

1 small red pepper, finely sliced into thin strips

Japanese soy sauce, to serve

MAKES 18 ROLLS

Sushi cones are a stylish way to serve sushi for a party, and the best way to use tiny Japanese mushrooms like hon-shigiri and enoki. Their delicate clusters of nodding heads would be completely lost in a rolled sushi.

sushi cones

4 sheets nori seaweed, halved (10 x 17 cm) and toasted over a gas flame or hotplate

½ recipe Vinegared Rice (page 11)

Japanese soy sauce, to serve

FILLINGS SUCH AS

enoki mushrooms, raw or smoked salmon, blanched asparagus, finely sliced carrot, cucumber strips, thin Japanese Omelette (page 121), sliced, sesame seeds, wasabi and Pickled Ginger (page 123)

MAKES ABOUT 20 ROLLS

1 Put a sheet of nori, shiny side down, on a work surface. Put 1 tablespoon rice on the left edge. Using wet hands, spread it lightly to cover half the seaweed completely.

2 Add your choice of filling ingredients diagonally across the rice, letting them overlap the top left corner.

3 To roll the cones, put one finger in the middle of the bottom edge, then roll up the cone from the bottom left, using your finger as the axis of the turn. As each cone is made, wet the outer edge with a finger dipped in vinegar, add a dot of rice to help seal it, then roll shut. Put on a serving platter with the join side down.

4 Serve with soy sauce for dipping.

VEGETARIAN ROLLS

Thick rolled sushi (*futo-maki*) are great for lunch, because they are more substantial than thin rolled ones (*hosi-maki*). However, they aren't ideal for fingerfood, because they are more than one mouthful.

five-colour roll

10 g dried gourd (kampyo)

2 teaspoons salt, for rubbing

250 ml dashi or fish stock

2 teaspoons Japanese soy sauce

2 teaspoons mirin (sweetened Japanese rice wine)

1 teaspoon sugar

1 recipe Japanese Omelette (page 121)

150 g spinach leaves, washed

3 sheets nori seaweed

½ recipe Vinegared Rice (page 11), divided into 3 portions

1 small red pepper, halved, deseeded and cut into fine strips

1 medium carrot, grated or very thinly sliced

HAND VINEGAR

4 tablespoons Japanese rice vinegar

250 ml water

a large frying pan, 28 cm diameter

a sushi rolling mat

MAKES 24 PIECES

1 Mix the hand vinegar ingredients in a small bowl and set aside.

2 Fill a bowl with water, add the gourd, rub it with salt, then drain and rinse thoroughly. Cover the gourd with fresh water and soak for 1 hour. Drain, then put in a saucepan, cover with boiling water and cook for 5 minutes. Drain, return to the pan, then add the dashi, 1 teaspoon of the soy, 1 teaspoon of the mirin and the sugar. Bring to the boil, reduce the heat and simmer for 5 minutes. Let cool in the liquid, then drain.

3 When the omelette is made, fold in the 4 sides, so they meet in the middle and the omelette is now double thickness and square. Remove to a board, let cool, then slice into 3 strips.

4 Wipe out and reheat the pan. Add the washed but still wet spinach and cover. Cook for 1½–2 minutes until wilted. Tip into a colander and let cool for a few minutes. Using your hands, squeeze out the liquid from the spinach.

5 Put 1 sheet of nori, rough side up with the long edge towards you, on a sushi rolling mat. Dip your fingers in the hand vinegar and spread with 1 portion of the rice, leaving 3 cm nori bare at the far edge. Put a strip of omelette in the middle and lay one-third of the gourd, spinach, pepper and carrot lengthways strips on top.

6 Pick up the mat from the near side and roll the mat following the method on pages 16–17. Wet the bare edge of nori and finish rolling to seal. Remove the mat and put the roll on a plate, join side down. Repeat to make 3 rolls, then cut each one into 8 pieces.

cucumber sushi

This simple, traditional sushi is a favourite with vegetarians.

1 sheet nori seaweed

1 recipe Vinegared Rice (page 11), divided into 2 portions

½ teaspoon wasabi paste

1 mini cucumber, deseeded and sliced lengthways

HAND VINEGAR

4 tablespoons Japanese rice vinegar

250 ml water

TO SERVE

Japanese soy sauce

Pickled Ginger (page 123)

wasabi paste

a sushi rolling mat

MAKES 12 PIECES

1 Mix the hand vinegar ingredients in a small bowl.

2 Toast the nori over a gas flame or hotplate and cut it in half. Put one piece on a sushi rolling mat.

3 Dip your hands in the hand vinegar and press each portion of rice into a cylinder shape. Put the cylinder on the piece of nori and spread it evenly over the sheet, leaving about 2 cm margin on the far side.

4 Brush ¼ teaspoon wasabi down the middle of the rice and put a line of cucumber on top.

5 Roll it up following the method on pages 16–17, then make a second roll using the remaining ingredients.

6 The sushi can be wrapped in clingfilm and left like this until you are ready to cut and serve.

7 To serve, cut in half with a wet knife and trim off the end (optional – you may like to leave a 'cockade' of cucumber sticking out the end). Cut each half in 3 and arrange on a serving platter. Serve with soy sauce, pickled ginger and wasabi paste.

This simple little roll makes a colourful addition to a sushi board. Try using a selection of different vegetables such as carrot, cucumber, radish, beetroot, and red, yellow or orange peppers.

bright vegetable and thin omelette rolls

3 large eggs

2 teaspoons Japanese soy sauce

2–3 teaspoons peanut oil

3 sheets nori seaweed, halved

½ recipe Vinegared Rice (page 1), divided into 6 portions

100 g mixed vegetables (see recipe introduction), shredded into fine matchsticks

1 teaspoon wasabi paste (optional)

HAND VINEGAR

4 tablespoons Japanese rice vinegar

250 ml water

a Japanese omelette pan or 20 cm frying pan

a sushi rolling mat

MAKES 36 PIECES

1 Mix the hand vinegar ingredients in a small bowl and set aside.

2 Put the eggs and soy sauce in a jug or bowl and beat well. Heat a film of oil in the pan and pour in one-third of the beaten egg mixture. Swirl the egg around to cover the base of the pan and cook for about 1 minute until set. Carefully remove the omelette to a plate and cook the remaining egg mixture in 2 batches. Cut each omelette in half.

3 Put a sheet of nori, rough side up with the long edge towards you, on a sushi rolling mat. Dip your hands in the hand vinegar and top the nori with 1 portion of the rice and piece of omelette (trim the end of the omelette if it hangs over the end of the rice). Arrange a line of vegetables along the edge closest to you and smear a little wasabi, if using, in a line next to the vegetables.

4 Carefully roll up, brushing a little water along the edge of the nori to seal if necessary. Repeat to make 6 rolls, then slice each roll into 6 even pieces.

grilled tofu roll

175 g silken tofu

2 tablespoons Japanese soy sauce

1 tablespoon mirin (sweetened Japanese rice wine)

1 teaspoon sugar

3 sheets nori seaweed, halved (you need 5 pieces, so you will have ½ sheet left over)

1 tablespoon white sesame seeds, toasted in a dry frying pan

1 tablespoon black sesame seeds

1 tablespoon oboro (dried pink fish flakes)

½ recipe Vinegared Rice (page 11), divided into 4 portions

1 teaspoon wasabi paste

HAND VINEGAR

4 tablespoons Japanese rice vinegar

250 ml water

a metal tray, lined with baking parchment

a sushi rolling mat

MAKES 24–32 PIECES

Silken tofu makes a moist, tender filling – I think that firm tofu can be a bit tough. To make silken tofu a little firmer, put it in a bowl and cover it with boiling water before you start making the sushi.

1 Mix the hand vinegar ingredients in a small bowl and set aside.

2 Cut the tofu into 1 cm square strips and arrange in a shallow dish. Put the soy sauce, mirin and sugar in a small bowl or jug and mix well. Pour the mixture evenly over the tofu and set aside to marinate for 10 minutes.

3 Preheat the grill. Place the tofu on a metal tray lined with baking parchment and grill for 2 minutes, turn the pieces over, brush with marinade and grill for a further 2 minutes. Set aside to cool.

4 Cut ½ sheet of nori into tiny shreds (about 3 mm), put in a small bowl and stir in the white and black sesame seeds and oboro.

5 Spread a sheet of clingfilm on top of the rolling mat. Put ½ sheet of nori on this. Dip your hands in the hand vinegar and spread with 1 portion of rice. Sprinkle with a quarter of the seed mixture, and press lightly into the rice.

6 Carefully lift the whole thing up and flip it over so the rice is face down on the clingfilm. Arrange slices of grilled tofu along the long edge of the nori closest to you, smear with a little wasabi paste and carefully roll up. Repeat to make 4 rolls, then slice each roll into 6–8 pieces.

7 Serve with extra wasabi and your choice of accompaniments.

One simple ingredient can make a perfectly elegant filling for rolled sushi. Here fresh green asparagus is marinated in white miso.

miso-marinated asparagus roll

1 Mix the hand vinegar ingredients in a small bowl and set aside.

2 Snap off any tough ends from the asparagus and discard. Bring a large saucepan of water to the boil, add the asparagus and simmer for 3–4 minutes until tender. Drain, rinse in plenty of cold water, then let cool.

3 If using medium asparagus, slice each piece in half lengthways to give 24 pieces. Arrange all the asparagus in a shallow dish.

4 Put the white miso paste, mirin and wasabi paste in a small bowl and mix well. Spread evenly over the asparagus and let marinate for 2–4 hours.

5 When ready to assemble the rolls, carefully scrape the marinade off the asparagus – it should be fairly clean, so the miso doesn't overwhelm the flavour.

6 Put ½ sheet of nori, rough side up with the long edge towards you, on a sushi rolling mat. Spread 1 portion of rice in a thin layer on the nori, leaving about 2 cm bare on the far edge.

7 Put 4 pieces of the asparagus in a line along the middle of the rice. Lift the edge of the mat closest to you and start rolling up the sushi away from you, pressing in the filling with your fingers as you roll. You may need a little water along the far edge to seal it. Repeat to make 6 rolls in all.

8 Using a clean, wet knife, slice each roll into 6 pieces and serve.

24 small or 12 medium asparagus spears

100 g white miso paste

2 teaspoons mirin (sweetened Japanese rice wine)

1 teaspoon wasabi paste

3 sheets nori seaweed, halved

½ recipe Vinegared Rice (page 11), divided into 6 portions

HAND VINEGAR

4 tablespoons Japanese rice vinegar

250 ml water

a sushi rolling mat

MAKES 36 PIECES

Mushrooms are a popular Japanese vegetable. Many of our regular supermarkets carry fresh shiitakes, and also may have enokis, like little clumps of white nails with tiny caps, and their bigger brothers, hon-shigiri, with brown 'berets' on their heads. If unavailable, use oyster and button mushrooms.

mushroom omelette sushi roll

100 g fresh shiitake mushrooms, about 12, stalks removed

100 g oyster mushrooms

50 g enoki mushrooms, roots trimmed

3 teaspoons peanut oil

1 tablespoon Japanese soy sauce

1 tablespoon mirin (sweetened Japanese rice wine)

2 eggs

¼ teaspoon salt

4 sheets nori seaweed

½ recipe Vinegared Rice (page 11), divided into 4 portions

HAND VINEGAR

4 tablespoons Japanese rice vinegar

250 ml water

a 23 cm frying pan, preferably non-stick

a sushi rolling mat

MAKES 24–32 PIECES

1 Mix the hand vinegar ingredients in a small bowl.

2 Slice the shiitake and oyster mushrooms into 1 cm slices. Separate the enoki mushrooms into bunches of two or three.

3 Heat 2 teaspoons of the oil in a large frying pan and sauté the shiitake and oyster mushrooms for 2 minutes, add the enoki and stir-fry for 1½ minutes. Add the soy sauce and mirin and toss to coat. Remove from the heat and let cool. Divide into 4 portions.

4 Put the eggs and salt in a bowl and beat well. Heat ½ teaspoon of the oil in a frying pan. Slowly pour in half of the egg, tipping the pan to get an even coating. Cook for about 1 minute until set, roll up, remove from the pan and let cool. Repeat with the remaining egg to make a second omelette. Slice the two rolled omelettes in half lengthways.

5 Put 1 sheet of nori, rough side up with the long edge towards you, on a sushi rolling mat. Dip your fingers in the hand vinegar. Spread with 1 portion of rice, leaving 3 cm of nori bare at the far edge. Put a strip of omelette down the middle and top with 1 portion of the mushrooms. Carefully roll up the nori in the mat, pressing the ingredients into the roll as you go. Wet the bare edge of nori and finish rolling to seal. Repeat to make 4 rolls.

6 Slice each roll into 6–8 pieces and serve.

inside-out avocado rolls with chives and cashews

Rolling inside-out sushi may seem a bit tricky, but it is actually very easy, because the rice on the outside moulds so well into shape, and it has the added bonus of looking spectacular.

2 small or 1 large ripe avocado

2 teaspoons lemon juice

2 tablespoons Japanese mayonnaise

¼ teaspoon sea salt

1 teaspoon wasabi paste (optional)

75 g cashew nuts, toasted (roasted, salted cashews work well)

a small bunch of chives

2 sheets nori seaweed, halved

½ recipe Vinegared Rice (page 11), divided into 4 portions

HAND VINEGAR

4 tablespoons Japanese rice vinegar

250 ml water

a sushi rolling mat

MAKES 24 PIECES

1 Mix the hand vinegar ingredients in a small bowl and set aside.

2 Peel the avocado and cut the flesh into small chunks. Toss in a bowl with the lemon juice, mayonnaise, salt and wasabi, if using. Mash slightly as you toss but not until mushy! Divide into 4 portions.

3 Chop the cashew nuts very finely and put in a bowl. Chop the chives very finely and mix with the cashew nuts. Divide into 4 portions.

4 Put a sheet of clingfilm on the rolling mat. Put ½ sheet of nori, rough side up with the long edge towards you, on a sushi rolling mat. Dip your fingers in the hand vinegar and spread 1 portion of rice over the nori.

5 Sprinkle 1 portion of the nut and chive mixture on top of the rice. Press it in gently with your fingers.

6 Carefully lift the whole thing up and flip it over so the rice is face down on the clingfilm. Remove the sushi mat. Put 1 portion of the avocado in a line along the long edge of the nori closest to you. Carefully roll it up, then cut in half, then each half into 3, giving 6 pieces. Repeat to make 4 rolls, giving 24 pieces.

pickled courgette roll
with beetroot sashimi

A thinly sliced ribbon of courgette makes a stunning alternative to nori on the outside of a sushi roll. It is easiest to cut the courgette and beetroot using a mandoline – the plastic Japanese ones are marvellous – but if you don't have one you can use a good sharp peeler or a sharp knife and a steady hand.

1 Mix the hand vinegar ingredients in a small bowl and set aside.

2 To make the pickling mixture, put the vinegar, sugar and mirin in a small saucepan and bring to the boil, stirring. Reduce to a simmer and cook for 5 minutes. Remove from the heat and let cool.

3 Thinly slice the courgettes lengthways, discarding the first and last couple of pieces (they will be too narrow). Arrange the slices flat in a shallow dish or container and pour the pickling mixture over the top. Set aside for 4 hours or overnight.

4 When ready to assemble the sushi, peel the raw beetroot and slice carefully, as thinly as possible.

5 Put the wasabi and mayonnaise in a small bowl and mix well.

6 Dip your fingers in the hand vinegar. Divide the seasoned rice into 18 portions about the size of a walnut, and shape each piece into a flattened ball. Wrap a ribbon of pickled courgette around the outside of each piece, top with a dab of wasabi mayonnaise and thin slivers of raw beetroot.

7 To make the dipping sauce, mix the soy sauce and sake together and serve in a small bowl beside the sushi.

3 medium courgettes
(green or yellow, or both)

1–2 very small beetroot or
5–6 baby beetroot, uncooked

1 teaspoon wasabi paste

1½ tablespoons Japanese
mayonnaise

½ recipe Vinegared Rice
(page 11)

PICKLING MIXTURE

250 ml Japanese rice vinegar

60 g sugar

2 tablespoons mirin (sweetened
Japanese rice wine)

HAND VINEGAR

4 tablespoons Japanese
rice vinegar

250 ml water

DIPPING SAUCE

2 tablespoons Japanese mild
soy sauce

1 tablespoon sake

MAKES 18 PIECES

PRESSED SUSHI

Battera, a speciality from Osaka, is one of the most popular sushi in Japan. It is made in a container or moulded into a log with a sushi mat and cut into small pieces. In restaurants and shops it often comes wrapped in a transparent sheet of kombu (dried kelp).

mackerel sushi pieces battera

1 medium very fresh mackerel, about 400 g, filleted

sea salt

3–4 tablespoons Japanese rice vinegar

½ recipe Vinegared Rice (page 11)

HAND VINEGAR

2 tablespoons Japanese rice vinegar

125 ml water

TO SERVE

Pickled Ginger (page 123)

Japanese soy sauce

a wooden mould or rectangular plastic container, 18 x 12 x 5 cm

MAKES 1 BATTERA: 16 PIECES

1 Start the preparation for this dish a few hours before cooking the rice. Take a dish larger than the fish fillets and cover with a thick layer of salt. Put the fillets, flesh side down, on top of the salt and cover completely with more salt. Set aside for 3–4 hours. Remove the mackerel and rub off the salt with damp kitchen paper. Carefully remove all the bones with tweezers, then put in a dish and pour the rice vinegar over the fillets. Let marinate for 30 minutes.

2 Mix the hand vinegar ingredients in a small bowl and set aside.

3 Using your fingers, carefully remove the transparent skin from each fillet, starting at the tail end. Put the fillets, skin side down, on a cutting board and slice off the highest part from the centre of the flesh so the fillets will be fairly flat. Keep the trimmings.

4 Line a wet wooden mould or rectangular container with a large piece of clingfilm.

5 Put a fillet, skin side down, in the mould or container. Fill the gaps with the other fillet and trimmings. Dip your fingers in the hand vinegar, then press the cooked rice down firmly on top of the fish. Put the wet wooden lid on top, or fold in the clingfilm and put a piece of cardboard and a weight on top.

6 You can leave it in a cool place (not the refrigerator) for a few hours. When ready to serve, remove from the container and unwrap any clingfilm. Take a very sharp knife and wipe it with a vinegar-soaked cloth or piece of kitchen paper. Cut the block of sushi in 4 lengthways, then in 4 crossways, making 16 pieces in all.

7 Arrange on a plate, and serve with pickled ginger and a little soy sauce in small individual dishes.

masu–zushi smoked fish sushi

Pressed sushi (*oshi-zushi*) like this, or log sushi (*bo-zushi*), will keep for up to 36 hours: as a result, they are the best-selling items at all Japanese airports. Travellers buy them for Japanese friends living abroad as a reminder of the true taste of Japan. They are easy to make and can be made the day before.

1 Mix the hand vinegar ingredients in a small bowl and set aside.

2 Arrange the smoked trout or salmon slices evenly in the bottom of a wet wooden mould. Alternatively, use a rectangular container lined with a piece of clingfilm large enough for the edges to hang out over the edges.

3 Dip your fingers in the hand vinegar, transfer the vinegared rice into the mould and press it firmly and evenly over the surface and into the corners. Put the wet wooden lid on top. If using a plastic container, fold in the clingfilm to cover the rice and top with a piece cardboard just big enough to fit the container, and put a weight on top. Leave in a cool place (but never the refrigerator) for 2–3 hours or overnight.

4 When ready to serve, remove from the container and unwrap any clingfilm. Take a very sharp knife and wipe it with a vinegar-soaked cloth or piece of kitchen paper. Cut the block of sushi into 4 lengthways, then in 4 crossways, making 16 pieces.

5 Arrange on a large serving plate. Put a fan-shaped piece of lemon on top. Serve with pickled ginger and a little soy sauce.

½ recipe Vinegared Rice (page 11)

HAND VINEGAR

2 tablespoons Japanese rice vinegar

125 ml water

TOPPINGS

150 g smoked rainbow trout or smoked salmon, thickly sliced

2 slices lemon, cut into 16 fan-shaped pieces

TO SERVE

Pickled Ginger (page 123)

Japanese soy sauce

a wooden mould or rectangular plastic container, 18 x 12 x 5 cm

MAKES 1 BLOCK: 16 PIECES

Just like cookies, these children's sushi are made in pretty colours and shapes. Specially shaped moulds are sold in Japanese stores, but if you don't have access to such exciting shops, use decorative cookie cutters and other mould shapes.

stars, hearts and flowers

1 To prepare the cherry blossom sushi, put the fish in a saucepan, add just enough boiling water to cover and simmer until well cooked. Drain, then carefully remove all the small bones. Pat dry with kitchen paper and return to the dry saucepan. Using a fork, crush into fine flakes. Add the sugar and a pinch of salt, then cook over low heat, continuously stirring with a fork, for about 2 minutes, or until the fish is very dry and flaky. If using food colouring, dilute 1 drop with 1 tablespoon water, then stir quickly through the fish to spread the colour evenly. Remove from the heat and let cool. (Alternatively, use fresh salmon cooked to flakes in the same way or crush canned cooked red salmon into flakes.)

2 To make the spring green sushi, bring a small saucepan of lightly salted water to the boil, add the peas and cook for 5 minutes or until soft. Drain and pat dry with kitchen paper. Purée in a food processor to form a smooth paste. Stir in the sugar and a pinch of salt.

3 To make the golden star sushi, lightly oil a small saucepan and put over moderate heat. Put the eggs, milk and sugar in a bowl, mix, then pour into the pan. Quickly stir with a fork to make soft scrambled eggs. Remove from the heat and let cool.

4 To assemble the cherry blossom sushi, put 1 tablespoon of the pink fish flakes in a small heart-shaped mould and press about 1 tablespoon of the rice on top. Turn out onto a plate, fish side up. Repeat until all the pink flakes and a third of the rice are used. Using a second mould, repeat using the green pea paste and another third of the rice. Using a third mould, repeat using the scrambled eggs with the remaining third of the rice. If using grilled fresh salmon, use a fourth mould.

5 Arrange all the sushi on a large plate and serve.

½ recipe Vinegared Rice (page 11), divided into 3 portions

CHERRY BLOSSOM SUSHI

100 g cod or haddock fillet, skinned

2 tablespoons sugar

sea salt

red vegetable food colouring*

SPRING GREEN SUSHI

100 g shelled green peas

2 teaspoons sugar

salt

GOLDEN STAR SUSHI

2 eggs, beaten

1 tablespoon milk

1 tablespoon sugar

oil, for cooking

star, daisy and diamond or heart shaped sushi moulds, or cookie cutters

MAKES 18–20 PIECES

* If you don't want to use food colouring, use grilled fresh salmon, flaked, instead of the white fish and colouring.

eggcup sushi

Hand moulding of rice is rather a messy job and it's also difficult to make identical shapes and sizes. Using an eggcup as a mold is a simple solution. These sushi are easy to make, pretty to serve and delicious to eat.

5–6 smoked salmon slices, about 125 g, halved to make 10–12 pieces

¼ recipe Vinegared Rice (page 11)

lemon or lime wedges, to serve

HAND VINEGAR

4 tablespoons Japanese rice vinegar

250 ml water

a small eggcup

MAKES 10–12 PIECES

1 Mix the hand vinegar ingredients in a small bowl and set aside.

2 Line an eggcup with clingfilm so it hangs over the edge of the cup. Line the whole cup with a piece of smoked salmon, filling any gaps with small pieces of salmon. Dip your fingers in the hand vinegar and put 1 tablespoon of the vinegared rice in the cup and press down gently with your thumbs. Do not overfill. Trim the excess salmon from the rim. Lift up the clingfilm and turn out the moulded sushi, upside down, onto a plate. Repeat to make 10 pieces.

3 Serve on a large platter with lemon or lime wedges.

Variation

Make soft scrambled eggs using 2 eggs, 1 teaspoon sugar and a pinch of salt. Let cool. Line the eggcup with clingfilm. Put 1 teaspoon of the scrambled eggs on the bottom. Gently press to make a firm base – the egg should come about half-way up the side of the cup. Put 1 tablespoon of vinegared rice on top of the egg and again gently press down with your thumbs. Do not overfill. Using the clingfilm, turn out the moulded sushi, upside down, onto a plate. Repeat this process for the remainder of the egg and rice. Serve with a tiny bit of red caviar on top.

BAGS, BOWLS AND BOXES

Gomoku-zushi means 'five-kinds sushi' and usually has 5–8 ingredients. This standard mixture is a popular dish for lunch because it's easy to cook and adjust the volume – and produces a relaxed atmosphere.

lunchbox sushi mixture

1 recipe Vinegared Rice (page 11)

TOPPINGS

3–4 dried shiitake mushrooms

6 tablespoons sugar

3 tablespoons Japanese soy sauce

½ carrot, finely sliced into 2 cm strips

200 ml chicken stock or water

1 tablespoon sake

50 g green beans, trimmed

½ small lotus root (renkon), (optional)

200 ml Japanese rice vinegar

2 eggs, beaten

sea salt

sunflower oil, for frying

SERVES 4–6

1 Soak the shiitakes in warm water for 30 minutes. Drain, retaining the soaking liquid. Remove and discard the stems, then thinly slice the caps. Put in a small saucepan, cover with 100 ml soaking liquid, 2 tablespoons sugar and 2 tablespoons soy sauce. Simmer for 10 minutes or until most of the liquid disappears. Transfer to a bowl and let cool.

2 Put the carrot in a saucepan with water to cover. Bring to the boil, then drain in a colander. Put the chicken stock or water in the pan, add the remaining soy sauce and sake, bring to the boil, add the carrot and cook for 3–4 minutes. Transfer to a bowl and let cool.

3 Add some lightly salted water to the saucepan, bring to the boil, add the beans and boil for 2 minutes until just soft. Drain and cool under running water. Pat dry with kitchen paper and slice diagonally into 5 cm long shreds.

4 Peel the lotus root, if using, and slice into thin rings. Bring a small saucepan of water to the boil, add 1 tablespoon rice vinegar and the lotus root and boil until just soft. Drain and transfer to a mixing bowl. Put the remaining rice vinegar in the saucepan, add the remaining sugar and 2 teaspoons salt, bring to the boil and stir until dissolved. Remove from the heat, add to the lotus root and let marinate for 15–20 minutes.

5 Beat the eggs with a pinch of salt. Heat a frying pan, brush with sunflower oil, add the egg and cook until just set. Transfer the egg pancake to a cutting board and cut into fine shreds, 5 cm long.

6 Put the rice in a bowl and fold in all the ingredients except the egg shreds and a few of the beans. Transfer to bowls or lunchboxes, top with the egg shreds and beans and serve.

A *fukusa* is an elaborate napkin used for the traditional Japanese tea ceremony. It is folded in various ways and is an important part of the classic performance. It has lent its name to this folded pancake sushi.

omelette parcel sushi
fukusa-zushi

1 Mix the hand vinegar ingredients in a small bowl and set aside.

2 Put the eggs in a large mixing bowl and lightly beat with a fork. Strain through a sieve into another bowl. Add the sugar, salt and blended cornflour and mix well until dissolved. Do not whip.

3 Heat the frying pan, add a little oil and spread over the base with kitchen paper. Add 1 small ladle of the egg mixture and spread evenly by tilting the pan. Cook over low heat for 30 seconds on each side until it becomes firm but not browned. Transfer to a plate and let cool. Repeat to make 8 egg pancakes.

4 Put the sesame seeds in a small saucepan and toss over moderate heat until they start to pop. Remove from the heat and crush coarsely with a mortar and pestle.

5 While the rice is still warm, fold in the chopped anchovies and crushed sesame seeds. Dip your hands in the hand vinegar, then divide the rice mixture into 8 balls.

6 Put an egg pancake on a board and put a rice ball in the centre. Fold the front of the pancake over the rice, then fold over the two sides, then the far side, like an envelope. Tuck the edges into the sides. Repeat to make 8 parcels. Alternatively, fold into a money bag, as shown (inset).

7 If using mizuna to tie the parcels, soak the stems in boiling water for about 30 seconds, using 2 pieces per parcel. Serve with pickled ginger and soy sauce.

10 eggs, beaten

2 tablespoons sugar

½ teaspoon sea salt

1 teaspoon cornflour blended with 1 teaspoon water

2 tablespoons sesame seeds (black or white)

½ recipe Vinegared Rice (page 11)

50 g anchovy fillets, finely chopped

1 bunch of mizuna (optional)

sunflower oil, for frying

HAND VINEGAR

4 tablespoons Japanese rice vinegar

250 ml water

TO SERVE

Pickled Ginger (page 123)

Japanese soy sauce

20 cm non-stick frying pan

MAKES 8 PARCELS

tofu bags inari-zushi

An *inari* is a shrine dedicated to agriculture and the fox is regarded as the envoy of the god. People used to offer fried beancurd (*abura-age*) to the fox; hence this special name. This sushi makes an ideal picnic lunch and children's snack.

1 Mix the hand vinegar ingredients in a small bowl and set aside.

2 Put the fried beancurd on a cutting board and roll each one with a rolling pin. This separates the thin layers inside the beancurd, making a bag. Put the beancurd in a mixing bowl, pour over boiling water, then drain – this will reduce the oiliness.

3 Cut each piece in half and carefully open each piece from the cut side (if not opened already), to make a bag.

4 Put the chicken stock or water in a saucepan, add 2 tablespoons of the sugar and bring to the boil. Add the beancurd bags, cook for 3 minutes on moderate heat, then add 1 tablespoon mirin and 1 tablespoon soy sauce. Simmer over a low heat for 10 minutes or until all the liquid disappears. Remove from the heat and transfer to a plate.

5 Meanwhile, soak the dried shiitakes in a bowl of warm water for at least 30 minutes, then drain, reserving the liquid. Cut off the stems and finely chop the caps. Pour 50 ml of the soaking liquid into a saucepan, add the remaining sugar, mirin and soy sauce, and the sake, if using, and bring to the boil. Add the carrot and shiitakes and simmer for 3–4 minutes until almost all the liquid is absorbed. Remove from the heat and let cool.

6 While the rice is still warm, fold in the cooked carrot and shiitakes. Dip your hands in the hand vinegar and divide the rice mixture into 6 balls. Squeeze out excess juice from the beancurd bags and open with your fingers. Stuff a ball of rice into each bag and fold in the edge (optional). You may cut some bags in half and stuff rice in the corner to make a 3-cornered 'Napoleon's hat' shape.

7 Arrange the bags on a serving plate and serve with pickled ginger and soy sauce.

½ recipe Vinegared Rice (page 11)

3 fresh Japanese fried beancurd (abura-age)

200 ml chicken stock

3 tablespoons sugar

2 tablespoons mirin (sweetened Japanese rice wine) or sweet sherry

2 tablespoons Japanese soy sauce

2 dried shiitake mushrooms

5 cm carrot, finely chopped

1 tablespoon sake (optional)

HAND VINEGAR

4 tablespoons Japanese rice vinegar

250 ml water

TO SERVE

Pickled Ginger (page 123)

Japanese soy sauce

MAKES 6 TOFU BAGS

stuffed squid sushi ika-zushi

Meat is rarely used in sushi, but this sweet, dry-cooked minced meat goes well with vinegared rice. It can be eaten as it is, or used as a stuffing for squid and served as an unusual party canapé. If you don't like to use meat, just use the squid flaps and tentacles in the sumeshi mixture, but reduce the amount of cooking juice accordingly.

1 Mix the hand vinegar ingredients in a small bowl and set aside.

2 Peel the outer skin off the squid. It comes off easily if you hold the 2 flaps together and peel down the body. Put the 2 squid tubes in a saucepan, add 1 tablespoon sake, cover with boiling water and simmer for 1–2 minutes. Do not overcook. Drain, rub the surface with a damp cloth to remove any marks, then sprinkle with the rice vinegar all over to retain the whiteness. Chop the flaps and tentacles.

3 Put the remaining sake, the sugar, mirin and soy sauce in a saucepan, mix and bring to the boil over moderate heat. Add the minced chicken or beef, the chopped squid flaps and tentacles and the chopped ginger, then stir vigorously with a fork until the meat turns white. Using a slotted spoon, transfer the cooked meat to another bowl, leaving the juice in the saucepan. Boil the juice over high heat for 1–2 minutes until thickened. Stir the meat back into the saucepan to absorb the juice, then remove from heat.

4 Make the vinegared rice and while still warm fold in the dry-cooked meat. Dip your fingers in the hand vinegar. Tightly stuff each squid body with half the rice mixture and slice crossways into 5–6 pieces with a sharp knife.

5 Arrange on plates and serve with pickled ginger.

2 medium squid, cleaned

3 tablespoons sake

2–3 tablespoons Japanese rice vinegar

2 tablespoons sugar

1 tablespoon mirin (sweetened Japanese rice wine) or sweet sherry

2 tablespoons Japanese soy sauce

50 g minced chicken or beef

2 cm fresh ginger, peeled and finely chopped

⅔ recipe Vinegared Rice (page 11)

Pickled Ginger (page 123), to serve

HAND VINEGAR

4 tablespoons Japanese rice vinegar

250 ml water

MAKES 10–12 PIECES

sushi in a bowl edomae chirashi-zushi

A bowl of sushi with sashimi on top is a favourite in Tokyo. You can use just one ingredient like tuna, or the assorted sashimi normally used in restaurants, including tuna, prawn, eel, sea bass, shellfish, herring roe, salmon roe – almost any good material from the market on the day. My selection is good for serving at home.

1 Bring a saucepan of lightly salted water to the boil, add the prawns and poach for 1–2 minutes until just pink. Remove with a slotted spoon, cool under running water, then pat dry with kitchen paper.

2 Return the water to the boil, add the octopus tentacle and cook for 7–8 minutes. Drain and cool under running water. Pat dry with kitchen paper and slice diagonally into thin discs.

3 Cut the fish into 4 slices each.

4 Put the squid, skin side up, on a cutting board and make very fine slits two-thirds of the way through the thickness, first lengthways, then crossways. Put in a bowl, pour over boiling water and drain. As the squid curls up, the slits open to form a flower. Immediately plunge into cold water. Pat dry with kitchen paper and cut into 4 bite-sized pieces.

5 Soak the shiitakes in warm water for 30 minutes and drain, retaining the soaking liquid. Cut off the stems and put in a saucepan with the sugar, mirin and a pinch of salt. Cover with some of the soaking liquid, stir, bring to the boil and simmer for 4–5 minutes until most of the liquid disappears. Let cool in the liquid.

6 Cut 2 green slices off the cucumber, 5 cm wide. Make fine slits lengthways, leaving 1 cm intact on one side. Open up the slits to make 2 cucumber fans.

7 Mix the hand vinegar ingredients in a small bowl.

8 Dip your fingers in the hand vinegar and divide the rice between 2 bowls and arrange the seafood over the rice and top with a cucumber fan and a pile of pink pickled ginger. Serve on small individual plates with wasabi and a little jug of soy sauce.

½ recipe Vinegared Rice (page 11)

SASHIMI: YOUR CHOICE OF

2 uncooked tiger prawns, peeled but with tail fins intact

1 octopus tentacle

125 g fresh tuna and/or salmon

1 turbot fillet, about 75 g

1 small squid, cleaned and skinned

2 large dried shiitake mushrooms

1 teaspoon sugar

1 teaspoon mirin (sweetened Japanese rice wine)

sea salt

HAND VINEGAR

4 tablespoons Japanese rice vinegar

250 ml water

TO SERVE

4 cm cucumber

Pickled Ginger (page 123)

wasabi paste

Japanese soy sauce

SERVES 2

a tub of spring sushi

1 recipe Vinegared Rice
(page 11)

RADISH PETALS

4–5 radishes, trimmed

2 tablespoons Japanese
rice vinegar

2 tablespoons sugar

EGG PETALS

1 egg, beaten with
a pinch of sea salt

¼ teaspoon cornflour mixed
with a little water

sunflower oil, for frying

YOUR CHOICE OF

5 dried shiitake mushrooms

5 tablespoons sugar

2½ tablespoons mirin
(sweetened Japanese
rice wine)

1 teaspoon Japanese
soy sauce

50 ml chicken stock

½ carrot, sliced into
2–3 cm matchsticks

25 g mangetout (snowpeas),
trimmed

75 g cod fillet

1 tablespoon sake

red vegetable food
colouring (optional)

3 tablespoons white sesame
seeds, lightly toasted
in a dry frying pan

200 g small prawns,
peeled and lightly cooked

sea salt

*flower cutters or a small
sharp knife*

SERVES 4–6

1 Cut a wedge out of each radish, then slice each radish crossways to form 5–6 petal shapes. Put the rice vinegar and sugar in a bowl and stir well until sugar has dissolved. Add the radish slices and marinate for a few hours or overnight. The red colour dissolves into the vinegar, making the slices cherry pink.

2 Mix the egg in a bowl with a pinch of salt and the blended cornflour. Heat a small frying pan, brush with the oil, add the egg mixture and cook until set. Using moulds or a small knife, cut out small shapes from the egg pancake such as hearts or petals.

3 Soak the shiitakes in warm water for 30 minutes, then drain, retaining the soaking liquid. Discard the stems and thinly slice the caps crossways. Put the shiitake slices, 100 ml from the soaking liquid and 2 tablespoons of the sugar in a saucepan, bring to the boil and cook for 3–4 minutes. Add the mirin and soy sauce, then simmer until the liquid disappears.

4 Put the chicken stock in a saucepan, add ½ teaspoon of the sugar, a pinch of salt and the carrot. Bring to the boil and cook for 2–3 minutes until just soft. Let cool in the juice.

5 Blanch the mangetout in lightly salted water. Slice diagonally into diamonds.

6 Bring a saucepan of water to the boil, add the cod, simmer for 3–4 minutes, then drain. Carefully remove the skin and all the bones. Return to a dry saucepan, add the sake, the remaining sugar and a pinch of salt. Using a fork, finely flake over low heat. If using red colouring, dilute it in a little water, then quickly stir to make a light pink *soboro* (fish flakes).

7 While the rice is still warm, fold in the shiitakes, carrot matchsticks, flaked fish, sesame seeds and prawns. Top with the radish and egg 'petals' and serve.

SASHIMI

Fresh fish is an absolute requirement for sashimi, so you should arrange with your fishmonger that the fish you are buying are fresh in on the day. Trendy fishmongers even fillet fish for sashimi for you, but it's best if you do it yourself just before serving.

classic sashimi

1 sea bream fillet
1 slice of lemon, cut into 8 fan-shaped wedges
1 small fresh mackerel
salt
Japanese rice vinegar
150 g tuna
150 g salmon fillet
1 small squid, cleaned and skinned
5 cm large daikon (white radish), peeled
iced water
4 shiso leaves (optional)

TO SERVE
4 teaspoons wasabi paste or powder
Japanese soy sauce

SERVES 4

1 Put the sea bream fillet on a cutting board, skin side down. Hold down the skin of the tail with your fingers, then run the blade along the skin, separating the flesh. Cut the whole fillet lengthways along the centre line. Insert the blade diagonally against the cutting board and slice each fillet crossways into 8 pieces, 1 cm thick. Make a slit in each piece and insert a fan-shaped piece of lemon.

2 Salt and vinegar the mackerel following the method on page 28. Slice the fillets into 1 cm pieces, as above.

3 Slice the tuna and salmon into 8 pieces, 6 x 3 x 1 cm thick.

4 Cut the squid into 8 pieces and finely slice each piece lengthways, leaving the pieces attached at one end.

5 Using a mandoline or sharp knife, finely shred the daikon. Put the shreds in a bowl of iced water for about 30 minutes to make them crisp. Drain and pat dry with kitchen paper.

6 To serve, put a mound of daikon shreds, a small mound of wasabi paste and a shiso leaf, if using, on each plate. Add 2 slices of each fish and serve with a small dish of Japanese soy sauce.

seared tuna
sashimi salad

You may take some time to get used to the idea of eating completely raw fish, but lightly blanched or seared fillet with salad is a good starting point. You can use other fish such as turbot, salmon or swordfish.

200 g fresh tuna or swordfish, skinned

iced water

green salad leaves

a small clump of enoki mushrooms, trimmed and separated

WASABI DRESSING

freshly squeezed juice of 1 lemon

2 teaspoons wasabi paste

1½ tablespoons Japanese soy sauce

SERVES 4

1 Grill the tuna or swordfish at a high heat for about 1 minute on each side until the surfaces are seared but the inside is still raw. Plunge into iced water. Drain and pat dry with kitchen paper. Slice into 5 mm thick pieces.

2 Mix the lemon juice, wasabi and soy sauce in a small bowl and set aside.

3 Arrange the salad leaves and enoki mushrooms in the centre of a large serving plate and arrange the seared fish over the leaves. Just before serving, pour the wasabi dressing over the top.

MISO SOUPS

A good dashi, or soup stock, is the basis for any great miso soup. A very simple version requires only kombu and water, but fresh and dried fish give an exceptional result. Little dried fish are sold in packets in Japanese and other Asian supermarkets. Many miso pastes come premixed with dashi, but these recipes call for pure miso paste – so check the packet. If you do have dashi included in your paste, replace the dashi quantity with water. Different qualities of miso paste will have different strengths, so adjust quantities according to taste.

japanese dashi and
combination miso soup

5 cm piece of kombu
(dried kelp)

1 tablespoon bonito flakes

COMBINATION MISO SOUP

2 tablespoons red miso paste

2 tablespoons white miso paste

MAKES 1.5 LITRES DASHI,
SOUP SERVES 4–6

1 To make the dashi, bring 3 litres water to the boil, add the kombu and bonito, return almost to the boil but do not let boil. Turn off the heat and let stand for 10 minutes. Strain and use immediately, or cool and store in the refrigerator for up to 2 days or freeze for up to 3 months.

2 To make the soup, put the red and white miso pastes in a small bowl. Add 4 tablespoons dashi and stir well.

3 Pour 1 litre dashi into a saucepan, bring to the boil, reduce to a simmer and stir in the miso mixture. Return to simmering point, but do not boil. Serve in small bowls. (Reserve the remaining dashi for another use.)

Miso pastes, widely used in Japanese soups, are made from soy beans, and so is tofu. There are many flavours and varieties of miso, but there are three main versions, with cultures based on barley, rice and soy beans. All are easy to find, either in the Japanese or sushi section of larger supermarkets, or in health food stores.

japanese miso soup

1 Remove the tofu from its container and slide it out onto a small plate. Put another plate on top and set aside for 30 minutes to press out some of the liquid.

2 Put the wakame in a bowl of water and let soften. Cut out any stiff sections with scissors and discard. Cut the wakame into 3 cm strips.

3 Put the dashi in a saucepan, bring almost to the boil, then reduce to a simmer. Set a strainer over the saucepan and add the miso. Using the back of a ladle, press the miso into the dashi and reduce the heat so the soup doesn't boil.

4 Add the wakame and simmer for 2 minutes.

5 Cut the tofu in half through its thickness. Cut into 1 cm cubes and drop into the soup (it is easier to do this if you hold the tofu cake in your palm and slice it carefully – it is very fragile). When the tofu floats to the surface, like ravioli, it is cooked. Carefully ladle into soup bowls, top with spring onion and serve.

Note This is the traditional accompaniment to sushi and similar dishes. The soup is drunk at the end – eat the tofu and wakame with chopsticks, then pick up the bowl and sip. (The rim and foot are specially designed not to be heat conductors, so you won't burn yourself.)

1 tub silken tofu

50 g wakame (dried seaweed)*

1 litre Dashi (page 109)

3 tablespoons dark miso paste

1 tablespoon white miso paste

1 spring onion, chopped

SERVES 4

*Japanese ingredients are now widely available, but if you can't find wakame, a few sprigs of watercress would taste delicious.

The more mellow flavours of white miso make a perfect drink to serve with sushi rolls – the delicious and delicate taste of this soup will not overpower even the most subtle of sushi.

white miso soup
with wakame, tofu and lettuce

5 g dried wakame seaweed

1 litre Dashi (page 109)

4 tablespoons white miso paste

100 g silken tofu, cut into small cubes

¼ iceberg or other crisp lettuce, finely sliced (optional)

SERVES 4

1 Soak the wakame in a bowl of hot water for 15 minutes, then drain.

2 Pour the dashi into a saucepan, bring to the boil, then reduce to simmering. Mix the miso paste in a bowl with a few tablespoons of the dashi to loosen it, then stir it into the simmering stock. Add the tofu and wakame and cook in the soup for 1 minute.

3 Divide the lettuce, if using, between 4 bowls, ladle the hot soup over the top, then serve.

red miso soup
with pork and noodles

This heartier version of miso soup is perfect at the
beginning or end of a sushi meal. Serve it before
heavier meat- or poultry-based sushi rolls or after
delicate fish or vegetarian rolls. It can also be beefed
up with stir-fried vegetables to serve as soup for two.

200 g soba
(buckwheat) noodles

1 litre Dashi (page 109)

1 small leek, finely sliced

3 tablespoons red miso paste

100 g roast pork, thinly sliced

SERVES 4

1 Fill a large saucepan three-quarters full of water
and bring to the boil. Add the soba noodles and
return the liquid to the boil. Add 1 cup of cold water
and bring to the boil again. Boil for 3 minutes,
drain, rinse in cold water and drain again.

2 Pour the dashi stock into a saucepan and bring
to the boil. Add the leeks and reduce to a simmer.
Mix the miso paste in a bowl with a few tablespoons
of the dashi to loosen it, then stir it into the
simmering stock.

3 Divide the noodles and slices of roast pork between
4 bowls, ladle over the hot soup, then serve.

You need only about one-third of this batter for the recipe, but half an egg seems difficult to work with, so use the rest of the batter for tempura vegetables or prawns. Alternatively, you could use the pressed croutons sold in Japanese shops.

red miso soup
with spring onions and
tempura croutons

1 litre Dashi (page 109)

3 tablespoons red miso paste

2 spring onions, finely sliced

TEMPURA CROUTONS

1 egg, separated

1 tablespoon lemon juice

150 ml iced water

60 g plain flour

peanut or safflower oil, for frying

SERVES 4

1 To make the batter, put the egg yolk, lemon juice and iced water in a bowl. Whisk gently, then whisk in the flour to form a smooth batter. Do not overmix.

2 Whisk the egg white in a second bowl until stiff but not dry, then fold into the batter.

3 To cook the croutons, fill a large wok or saucepan one-third full with oil and heat to 190°C (375°F), or until a small cube of bread turns golden in 30 seconds.

4 Carefully drop teaspoons of the batter into the oil and cook for 30 seconds until crisp. Scoop out and drain on kitchen paper.

5 Pour the dashi into a saucepan, bring to the boil, then reduce to a simmer. Mix the miso paste with a few tablespoons of the dashi to loosen it, then stir into the simmering stock. Divide the stock between 4 bowls, add the croutons and spring onions and serve.

There are three main kinds of Japanese soups: the miso soups with tofu and wakame served as a 'drink' with sushi or sashimi; the big soups, such as New Year Soup; and these – clear dashi in which floats one to three beautiful ingredients, each a complement to the other.

clear japanese soup
with prawns, citrus and pepper

4 shelled medium uncooked prawns, tail fins intact

4 thin strips of citrus peel, such as yuzu if available, tied in a knot, or a slice of carrot or other vegetable, blanched

1 litre Dashi (page 109), hot but not boiling, or 1 litre hot water with dashi powder

4 leaves of Japanese herb, such as shiso, or a slice of spring onion

furikake seasoning, Japanese seven-spice, or black pepper, to serve

SERVES 4

1 Cut each prawn along the belly without cutting all the way through. Open out flat. Make a small slit where the backbone would be if it were a fish. Thread the tail up and through the slit in the back, then fan out the tail fins.

2 Cut the citrus zest with a cannelle cutter or a small sharp knife. Put the zest and prawns in a bowl and pour over boiling water.

3 Put the hot dashi in 4 Japanese soup bowls, add 1 prawn, a knot of zest or a piece of carrot and a shiso leaf or a slice of spring onion. Put on the lid, then serve with a small dish of furikake seasoning, Japanese seven-spice or black pepper.

BASICS

This is the basic method for cooking Japanese omelette. It is a regular breakfast item as well as being used for sushi.

japanese omelette
tamago yaki

1 Using a fork, beat the eggs and egg yolk and strain through a sieve into a bowl. Add the sugar, soy sauce and pinch of salt and stir well until the sugar has dissolved. Do not whisk or make bubbles.

2 Heat a Japanese omelette pan or frying pan over moderate heat and add a little oil. Spread evenly over the base by tilting the pan, then wipe off any excess oil with kitchen paper, at the same time making sure the surface is absolutely smooth. Keep the oiled paper on a plate.

3 Reduce the heat and pour one-third of the egg mixture evenly over the base by tilting the pan. If large air bubbles pop up immediately, the pan may be too hot – if so, remove the pan from the heat and put it back on when the egg starts to set.

4 Prick any air bubbles with a fork and when the egg is about to set with chopsticks or a fork, to roll the egg layer 2–3 times from one side to the other. Oil the empty base of the pan with the oiled paper and push the rolled egg back to the other side.

5 Again using the oiled paper, brush the base of the pan, then pour half the remaining egg mixture evenly over the base by tilting the pan and lifting the egg roll so the egg mixture flows underneath.

6 When the egg starts to set, roll again, using the first roll as the core. Repeat this oiling and rolling using up the remaining egg mixture. Remove from the pan and let cool before cutting.

4 eggs
1 egg yolk
2½ tablespoons sugar
1 teaspoon Japanese
soy sauce
sea salt
1–2 tablespoons sunflower oil

*a Japanese omelette pan
or 20 cm non-stick frying pan*

chopsticks or a fork

MAKES 1 OMELETTE

mixed pickles

Other vegetables can be pickled and served with sushi alongside ginger. They look wonderfully colourful, adding a touch of drama to your sushi platter and making it appear very professional.

½ cucumber, about 10 cm long

1 carrot, about 100 g

100 g daikon (mooli or white radish), peeled, or 6 red radishes

¼ small green cabbage, about 150 g

6 garlic cloves, finely sliced

1 tablespoon sea salt

½ lemon, sliced

250 ml Japanese rice vinegar

175 g sugar

MAKES ABOUT 500 ML

1 Cut the cucumber in half lengthways and scoop out the seeds. Slice the cucumber, carrot and daikon into very thin strips.

2 Slice the cabbage into 1 cm strips. Put all the vegetables and garlic in a colander, sprinkle with salt and toss well. Set aside for 30 minutes, then rinse thoroughly and top with the sliced lemon.

3 Put the rice vinegar and sugar in a saucepan with 60 ml water. Bring to the boil, stirring until the sugar has dissolved. Boil for 5 minutes. Let cool, then pour over the vegetables and lemon. Cover and refrigerate for at least 24 hours or until needed. Keeps for 1 month in the refrigerator.

pickled ginger gari

Pickled ginger is the traditional companion for sushi. The subtle flavouring of raw fish, delicate rice and fresh vegetables can easily be overpowered by the lingering flavours of previous morsels. Ginger helps cleanse the palate, introducing a sharp freshness that stimulates the taste buds for the next delight.

1 Peel the ginger and slice it very finely with a mandoline or vegetable peeler. Put it in a large sieve or colander and sprinkle with salt. Set aside for 30 minutes, then rinse thoroughly.

2 Put the rice vinegar and sugar in a saucepan, add 60 ml water and bring to the boil, stirring until the sugar has dissolved. Boil for 5 minutes. Let cool, then pour over the ginger. If you would like it to be pink, like shop-bought ginger, add the beetroot, radish or food colouring. Cover and refrigerate for at least 24 hours or until needed.

150 g piece of fresh ginger

1 tablespoon sea salt

125 ml Japanese rice vinegar

115 g sugar

1 slice fresh beetroot, 1 red radish, sliced, or a drop of red food colouring (optional)

MAKES ABOUT 250 ML

wasabi paste

Most of the wasabi we buy in tubes is a mixture of horseradish and wasabi – or it can be just horseradish dyed green. If you buy wasabi paste from a Japanese market, you will have a selection of various qualities, and it is always preferable to buy the best.

Many Japanese cooks prefer to mix their own paste from silver-grey wasabi powder, sold in small cans, like paprika, believing that the flavour is stronger and sharper.

The fresh roots are not widely available, even in Japan, but if you see them in a specialist greengrocer's, sold on a bed of ice, do try them. To experience the real flavour and rush of wasabi you can make your own paste from them. It was traditionally grated using a sharkskin grater, but a porcelain ginger grater or a very fine abrasive zester will also work. After grating, the heat in wasabi lasts for only about 10 minutes, so you must use it straight away.

wasabi from powder

1 teaspoon wasabi powder

SERVES 1

Put the wasabi powder in a small bowl, such as an eggcup. Add 1 teaspoon water and mix with the end of a chopstick. Serve immediately.

fresh wasabi paste

1 fresh wasabi root

a wasabi grater or ginger grater

SERVES 6–8

Scrape or peel off the rough skin from the wasabi root. Using a circular motion, rub the wasabi gently against an abrasive grater onto a chopping board. Pound and chop the grated wasabi to a fine paste with a large knife or cleaver. Eat within 10 minutes.

Note To stop wasabi discolouring for as long as possible, turn the little bowl upside down until serving – this will stop the air getting at it.

index

photography credits

Martin Brigdale: 31

Peter Cassidy: 1–4, 6–22, 33, 35, 42–44, 47–51, 57–61, 70, 77, 81, 84–107, 111, 113, 119–121, 128

William Lingwood: 66, 71, 73

Diana Miller: 5, 25–30, 34, 37–41, 45, 52–56, 62–65, 68, 72, 75–76, 79–80, 83, 108, 112, 115–116, 122–125

Simon Walton: 67

Simon Wheeler: 114